Strategies and Resources for Teaching and Learning in Inclusive Classrooms

Strategies and Resources for Teaching and Learning in Inclusive Classrooms

Paul Gardner

David Fulton Publishers
London

David Fulton Publishers Ltd
The Chiswick Centre, 414 Chiswick High Road, London W4 5TF

www.fultonpublishers.co.uk

First published in Great Britain 2002 by David Fulton Publishers

British Library Cataloguing in Publication Data
A catalogue record for this book is available from the British Library.

ISBN 1 85346 711 1

Typeset by Textype Typesetters, Cambridge
Printed in Great Britain by Bell and Bain Ltd, Glasgow

Contents

Introduction

'The world is in a terrible state of chassis.'

Juno and the Paycock

The final stage of this book was written against a background of international tension. It is post 11 September 2001, a date interpreted by different commentators as both a heinous crime against humanity and a symbolic challenge to the hegemony of the United States of America. The dominant political discourse of the day suggests that religious difference and ethnicity were at the heart of conflict. At a more parochial level, we have seen the eruption of riots and inter-ethnic gang fights in British towns and cities: Oldham, Burnley and Bradford. Fuelled by mistrust, prejudice and racism, racial attacks on Muslims and anyone who appears to be Muslim increased after mid-September. As Sean O'Casey's comic character, Jockser Daly, says, the world does indeed seem to be 'in a terrible state of chassis'. Given such a bleak scenario, it would be easy to fall into a pit of pessimism about the future of our multicultural society; but we should not give way to appearances, no matter how powerful they may be. There are alternative discourses, ones that offer hope. Imagine, a Christmas day, two children are about to open their presents, which lie under the Christmas tree in the corner of the room, glinting with tinsel. The television is on and morning prayers are read. There is nothing remarkable about this scene; it was the secular celebration of a Christian festival, and one that was being replicated in millions of homes across the country. But two things did make this scene different. One was the fact that the prayers being broadcast were on Panjab Radio; they were Sikh prayers. The other event was a phone call to the youngest child in the house. A classmate phoned her to wish her happy Christmas. Again, there is nothing remarkable about that, it is customary for friends and family to wish one another well at Christmas time. What made the phone call noteworthy was the fact that my daughter's friend is Muslim. So, here we have it, against a backdrop of apparent international and communal disorder an 11-year-old British-Muslim girl phones her British-Sikh friend to wish her well on the day of an important Christian celebration.

The scenario above did not make headline news and would not have come to the attention of anyone beyond my immediate family but for the fact that I am in the privileged position of being able to write for publication. In its own small way, this anecdote is a potent message for the future. It represents, if not a vision, then a glimpse of the potential for an inclusive society and inclusive world. At the heart of inclusion is the recognition that difference does not equal separateness and division. However, inclusion does not just happen: it has to be worked at, especially at times when world disorder suggests that it is an impossibility. Children, parents and teachers, as much as politicians and self-styled terrorist leaders, are makers of social reality. Through word and deed, players on small stages can weave narratives that bind lives together and imbue them with the kind of positive meanings that challenge larger and more discordant scenarios. These small narratives need systematic articulation in many ways and in various quarters if they are to acquire permanence and the strength to rival the potency of the larger ones.

Apart from the family, one social stage where meanings are established and maintained is school. As an agency of enculturation, school is one place where complex societies teach the young about themselves as social beings. Children learn from their teachers and each other, firstly about what there is in the world that is worthy of viewing and secondly about appropriate ways of how to view the world. The kinds of knowledge, concepts and skills learned in school contribute significantly towards the meanings children attribute to themselves and others. Within school itself, the classroom is the daily focus where this social 'reading' is most intense. It was for this reason that in the introduction to *Teaching and Learning in Multicultural Classrooms*, to which this book is a more practical sequel, I wrote:

> The classroom is a critical social arena where individual lives are shaped and influenced through attitudes and values, which are embedded in both the process and content of learning. High expectations, positive values and an inclusive ethos, that is, an acceptance and conceptual understanding of difference, are the guardians of success . . . They . . . influence self-worth, hope and optimism; the kind of emotional balance that leads to positive relationships built on empathy. (Gardner 2001: ix)

The imagery and language of the curriculum, the examples we use as teachers, the way we respond to the diverse interests, experiences and needs of our pupils, and the organisation of teaching and learning send powerful messages to pupils about what is valued and what is disregarded. Under the theme of inclusion, the National Curriculum establishes three principles to guide effective practice. These are:

- Setting suitable learning challenges.
- Responding to pupils' diverse needs.
- Overcoming potential barriers to learning and assessment for individuals and groups of pupils.

(DfEE/QCA 1999: 32–9)

The first of these principles refers to the involvement of all pupils in learning and the use of strategies to enable them to achieve the highest possible standard in their education. The second acknowledges the diverse experiences and understandings children bring to school. Such experiences and understandings are influenced by gender, social class, ethnicity, disability, etc., which act as powerful mediators in children's learning. Pupils need to feel psychologically, as well as physically, secure in school if they are to learn effectively and achieve success in their learning. This means that such things as cultural identity, religious beliefs, language and the general life experiences of pupils need to be an integral part of the curriculum. The third principle involves the creation of supportive learning environments in which resources, the language of instruction and teaching and learning strategies are used to maximise pupils' access to the curriculum.

Despite the grand design underpinning the drive for equal opportunities in the National Curriculum, the inclusion of linguistic, cultural and religious diversity does not appear to be a widespread feature of schools. Many teachers in exclusively white and predominantly white schools still appear impervious to the reality of multi-ethnic society (Gaine 1995; Jones 1999) and my own small-scale research suggests that the delivery of an inclusive curriculum is sparse even in some multi-ethnic schools (Gardner 2001: 27).

Following the Stephen Lawrence Inquiry racial equality is on the agenda of every public institution. The Race Relations (Amendment) Act 2000 places a duty on every state school in the country to take action to eradicate racial discrimination. Inclusion, access and achievement are part of the armoury of key words in the drive towards equality of opportunity in education.

In order to meet the new 'standards' for Qualified Teacher Status (QTS) published by the Teacher Training Agency (TTA 2002), students will need to be familiar with a repertoire of strategies for collaborative group work as well as to demonstrate their ability to enhance pupils' learning and achievement by means of collaborative working with other adults in the classroom.

Part One of this book addresses issues related to inclusion, equality of access and collaboration between adults in the classroom. A rationale for collaborative learning is made. By drawing upon my own practical experience of working collaboratively in multi-ethnic schools, primarily at Key Stages Two and Three, my intention in the second part of the book is to focus on the processes and content of learning that can form part of inclusive education. The strategies emphasise active and collaborative approaches to learning and draw upon the multicultural context of our society for their content. I acknowledge three major sources that have influenced their design. The first influence is the work of Douglas Barnes (1976), who drew attention to the educational benefits of exploratory talk through collaborative group work. The second is the work of Lunzer and Gardner (1979), who introduced Directed Activities Related to Texts (DARTs) as a means of encouraging pupils to read for meaning. The third influence is Stuart Scott, Director of the Collaborative Learning Project, who promoted the use of well planned group learning activities that enabled pupils with relatively little English to access the curriculum.

Underpinning the resources included here are generic learning strategies, which make them applicable to most, if not all, Key Stages. The materials can be photo-copied and used as they stand, but they are essentially ideas to be adapted to the particular needs of pupils and their teachers.

Part One

Inclusive classrooms:
Ethos and approaches

1 Principles of inclusion

According to statistics compiled by the Commission for Racial Equality (1998), Black pupils are five times more likely to be excluded from school than their White peers. Exclusion in the sense of physical removal from school is, however, only the tip of the iceberg. Some research suggests that prevailing attitudes and behaviour in some schools render Black and Asian children invisible. Based on extensive interviews with teachers, trainee teachers and lecturers in initial teacher education, Russell Jones (1999: 139–42) has devised a typology of disappearance, which describes the various strategies used to avoid 'race' and ethnicity in predominantly White schools. These strategies include the following;

- failure to see the 'race' or ethnicity of a pupil as a significant aspect of their identity;
- failure to address 'race' and ethnicity because it is someone else's responsibility or is covered by an official or quasi-official document;
- failure to recognise racism as a social problem because the problems faced by Black and Asian pupils are due to them as individuals;
- the view that issues to do with 'race' and ethnicity are of low priority in a teacher's work or that there is insufficient time to deal with them as issues;
- the view that to address issues of 'race', ethnicity and racism creates problems or only makes matters worse.

The conclusion is that some schools, notably those with relatively few Black and Asian pupils, whilst not physically excluding those pupils from school, in effect, symbolically exclude them by failing to recognise their ethnic identity. Issues and conflicts that arise in such schools linked to 'race' and ethnicity tend to be problematised around the individual rather than dealt with as socially constructed problems. In contrast, inclusive schools recognise the multiple identities of pupils and create school environments in which those identities are valued and respected. They offer support to those pupils who are harassed because of their identity and put in place strategies to challenge prejudice.

In contrast to Jones's work, Blair and Bourne (1998) identified ways in which 'race' and ethnicity are treated as transparent issues by successful multi-ethnic schools. The salient points emerging from their analysis show that effective schools have the following characteristics:

- headteachers who take a strong lead on equality issues;
- an emphasis on listening to, and acting upon, the experiences of pupils and their parents;
- strong links with parents and the local community;
- a concern for developing the 'whole' child, including the personal, social and

emotional as well as academic potential of individual pupils;

- an inclusive curriculum – one that works within the parameters of the National Curriculum to include a recognition of diverse linguistic, cultural, religious and ethnic identities;
- clear practices and procedures for dealing with and preventing racist bullying and harassment;
- the application of strategies to prevent the exclusion of pupils from school for both fixed and permanent periods;
- high expectations of both pupils and teachers supported by clear systems for targeting and monitoring the progress of individual pupils and cohorts of pupils, such as ethnic groups, to ensure equality of outcome.

Blair and Bourne emphasise that successful attempts to create inclusive education depend upon the application of a raft of measures rather than being dependent upon a single factor. In addition to studies of schools and their perceptions and practices in relation to 'race' and ethnicity, educationalists in the field of 'special education' have also identified important features of inclusive approaches. Some of the inclusive approaches in special education are also applicable to inclusive approaches for cultural diversity, since the intention is to find strategies that involve the whole school community. Ainscow (1999: 149) draws attention to the Index of Inclusion, which was devised by parents, teachers and representatives of disability groups. The Index is based on two sources of information: one is evidence from research into methods of improving participation of pupils previously excluded or marginalised, and the other is evidence of effective methods of school improvement. The Index establishes definitions of inclusion which can be accessed on the website of the Centre for Studies in Inclusive Education (www.inclusion.uwe.ac.uk/csiefaqs). In summary, the definitions state that inclusion

- involves the processes of increasing the participation of students in, and reducing their exclusion from, the cultures, curricula and communities of local schools;
- involves restructuring the cultures, policies and practices in schools so that they respond to the diversity of students in their locality;
- is concerned with the learning and participation of all students vulnerable to exclusionary pressures;
- is concerned with improving schools for staff as well as for students;
- views diversity not as a problem to be overcome, but as a rich resource to support the learning of all;
- is concerned with fostering mutually sustaining relationships between schools and communities;
- in education is one aspect of inclusion in society as a whole.

Further reading of the Index's three main dimensions reveals close parallels to Bourne and Blair's findings, which demonstrate the importance of drawing on all fields of research and practice in inclusive education. In essence, inclusive approaches begin with the recognition that our society and its schools are populated by people of diverse backgrounds and needs, and that historically some groups and some individuals have been excluded, either physically or symbolically. Inclusive approaches in education seek to change structures, practices and procedures as well

4

as behaviour to ensure that difference not only is accepted but is recognised for its educational value. As Kincheloe and Steinberg (1997: 43) acknowledge:

> individuals who belong to divergent socio-economic groups can learn much from one another if provided the space to exchange ideas and analyse mutual difficulties. As such a powerful force, difference must not simply be tolerated but cultivated as a spark to human creativity.

Of course, this point applies equally to differences of gender, religion, culture and 'race' as it does to socio-economic status.

Features of inclusive classrooms

Whilst recognising that inclusion is a multi-dimensional issue that must operate at all levels of school, my intention in this book is to focus on inclusion at the level of classroom practice. More specifically, I want to look at curriculum content and the organisation of learning and especially the use of resources that encourage collaborative learning. Collaborative learning is important to inclusive classroom organisation because it increases the opportunities pupils have to share their knowledge, including specific cultural knowledge. When pupils work together to achieve a collective goal they utilise and develop important communication and social skills. If the materials they use reflect cultural, religious and ethnic diversity in appropriate ways, not just of pupils within the classroom or school but of society as a whole, then significant messages are delivered to pupils about the positive value attributed by school to social and cultural diversity. In turn, a classroom ethos that encourages pupils to share their thoughts, ideas, knowledge and skills, led by teachers who elicit and who genuinely value the contributions of all pupils, is likely to generate the kind of social relationships which make pupils feel psychologically secure in their learning. The Index of Inclusion referred to above identifies a comprehensive range of indicators of inclusive cultures and practices that schools can use to evaluate their own performance in relation to inclusive education. Listed below are some of the specific indicators from the Index that can be applied to classroom practice.

- Everyone is made to feel welcome.
- Students help one another.
- Staff collaborate with one another.
- Staff and students treat one another with respect.
- High expectations are set for all pupils.
- Students are equally valued.
- Staff seek to remove all barriers to learning and participation in school.
- Lessons are responsive to student diversity.
- Lessons are made accessible to all students.
- Lessons develop an understanding of difference.
- Students are actively involved in their own learning.
- Students learn collaboratively.
- Assessment encourages the achievements of all students.
- Classroom discipline is based on mutual respect.
- Teachers plan, review and teach in partnership.
- Teachers are concerned to support the learning and participation of all students.

- Student difference is used as a resource for teaching and learning.
- Staff develop resources to support learning and participation.

One important feature of an inclusive classroom is the development of attitudes and cognitive resources that lead to open rather than closed perceptions of difference. In its discussion of 'Islamophobia' or anti-Muslim prejudice, the Runnymede Trust (www.runnymedetrust.org/beb/islamophobia/nature.html) has identified and contrasted eight sets of open and closed views of Islam. These views are set out in Table 1.1. Reactions following the events of 11 September 2001, which have led some people to conflate Islam with terrorism, give the discussion added significance and highlight the need for those with influence to model open attitudes to the religion and its adherents. What is stated under the heading of 'Open views of Islam' could be applied to any religious, cultural or ethnic group that is subject to prejudice and discrimination. Indeed, recognition that all groups are diverse within themselves must be a central concept in inclusion as is the acknowledgement that difference does not imply superior or inferior relations between groups and that different groups often share similarities, be those differences based on religion or some other marker of difference.

Table 1.1 Closed and open views of Islam

Distinctions	Closed views of Islam	Open views of Islam
1. Monolithic versus diverse	Islam is seen as a single monolithic bloc, static and unresponsive to new realities.	Islam is seen as diverse and progressive, with internal differences, debates and developments.
2. Separate versus interacting	Islam is seen as separate and other, i.e. (a) not having any aims or values in common with other cultures; (b) not affected by them; (c) not influencing them.	Islam is seen as interdependent with other faiths and cultures, i.e. (a) having certain shared values and aims; (b) affected by them; (c) enriching them.
3. Inferior versus different	Islam is seen as inferior to the West – barbaric, irrational, primitive, sexist.	Islam is seen as distinctively different, but not deficient or inferior and equally worthy of respect.
4. Enemy versus partner	Islam is seen as violent, aggressive, threatening, supportive of terrorism, engaged in a clash of civilisations.	Islam is seen as an actual or potential partner in joint cooperative enterprises and in the solution of shared problems.
5. Manipulative versus sincere	Islam is seen as a political ideology used for political or military advantage.	Islam is seen as a genuine religious faith, practised sincerely by its adherents.
6. Criticisms of West rejected versus considered	Criticisms made by Islam of the West are rejected out of hand.	Criticisms of the West and other cultures are considered and debated.
7. Discrimination defended versus criticised	Hostility towards Islam is used to justify discriminatory practices towards Muslims and the exclusion of Muslims from mainstream society.	Debates and disagreements with Islam do not diminish efforts to combat discrimination and exclusion.
8. Islamophobia seen as natural versus problematic	Anti-Muslim hostility is accepted as natural and normal.	Critical views of Islam are themselves subjected to critique, lest they be inaccurate and unfair.

2 EAL acquisition

The long-term needs of the EAL learner

Children who are learning English as an additional language (EAL) have already acquired comprehensive linguistic competence in a first and possibly second language before exposure to English. In the early years of EAL acquisition, English will be the child's weakest language, which is a problem for schools that are dependent upon achieving good SATs results, but in itself, the fact that English is the weaker language is not a problem. Providing the child has exposure to a rich, comprehensible diet of English, acquisition will occur. Cummins (1984) estimates that oral fluency in the social use of an additional language can be acquired within two years. However, it can take up to seven years for a child to become fully competent in the use of that language for cognitive and academic purposes. This time span has implications for the assessment of the bilingual child in English, which will remain her weaker language for a significant period of her school career. It also has implications for the duration and varying types of support needed by the child in order to achieve academic success through the medium of English. The Northern Association of Support Services for Equality and Achievement (NASSEA) has taken this into account in its assessment system for EAL pupils (see the Resources and Advice section). Reflecting Cummins's findings, this system incorporates the likelihood that the EAL learner may need additional support up to and including attainment at Levels 4 and 5 of the National Curriculum. When managing support, schools need to take account of the long-term needs of EAL learners in order to help pupils achieve their potential. Long-term support will be essential if schools are to realise their specific duties to achieve equality of opportunity under the Race Relations (Amendment) Act 2000.

The bilingual learner, language and education

It is estimated that 70 per cent of the world's population speaks two or more languages. A significant minority of the British population is either bi- or multi-lingual. But what does it mean to be bilingual? Some definitions of bilingualism imply the ability to speak two languages fluently. But it is probably quite rare for a speaker of two languages to speak them equally. This is because language use occurs in different contexts for different purposes. For example a British-Panjabi bilingual child who learns science in school through the medium of English is unlikely to use Panjabi to discuss scientific matters and concepts, but equally the same child may find it difficult to use any language other than Panjabi when talking to her parents about culturally specific matters. Bilingual speakers have access to a repertoire of linguistic resources in different languages. Choices about language use are influenced by a number of factors including the subject under discussion, the social setting and the relationship of the speaker to her audience. A working definition of bilingualism might be located around the use of two languages on a regular, if not daily, basis.

It is important that teachers recognise the EAL learners' linguistic skills and reflect these in the classroom. Language is an important signifier of personal, social and cultural identity, and recognition of the child's first language within the classroom is an equally powerful way of saying to the child, 'You are of value and so too is your cultural identity.' The use of different languages in the classroom conveys significant messages, therefore, for inclusion. If the teacher learns even a few phrases of the bilingual child's first language and uses them in the classroom, this acts as even more powerful reinforcement of inclusion. Quite simply the message is, 'You belong.' This is likely to make pupils feel psychologically secure in school, which is a key feature of Maslow's hierarchy of need in relation to motivation and achievement (Maslow 1968). Another reason for maintaining the child's first language has to do with cognitive development. Cognitive theories show how children refine their conceptual maps or schema through the processes of accommodation and assimilation, that is, the inclusion of new data into existing schema or the reframing of existing concepts in the light of new data and fresh realisation. For the EAL learner conceptual development began in the child's first language. If the first language is maintained whilst English is acquired, conceptual development is allowed to occur unhindered. Cummins shows that the deeper the conceptual development in one language the easier it is to acquire the signifiers (words) for those concepts in a second language. Some studies have been able to demonstrate that teaching through the medium of the child's first language has not only enabled the child's easier access to the curriculum but has actually improved their acquisition of English relative to a control group taught solely through the medium of English. Some countries have acknowledged the findings by implementing bilingual education. With the exception of Wales there has been no significant provision for bilingual education in Britain.

The process of acquiring an additional language

A distinction can be made between language learning and language acquisition. As children we acquire a first language. We are not conscious that we are learning language, because we are fully immersed within it. The child is driven by basic needs to communicate meaning. Through interactions with adults and other children, the young child gradually acquires the necessary sounds and sequences of sounds that make up the symbolic code of the language of their environment. Language learning, on the other hand, often occurs when we have acquired a first language. It involves the conscious learning of words and grammar, often in decontextualised contexts. At one time EAL support was thought beneficial in withdrawal groups, where the emphasis was on language learning. However, bilingual pupils need a combination of both language acquisition and language learning, but in differing degrees. The emergent bilingual child is immersed in a classroom environment where English is the main language. There is no need therefore for the child to be withdrawn from the classroom to be taught what is already the language of instruction. In the classroom bilingual learners are immersed in curriculum-related language. The learning objectives of the lesson remain the focus for learning, whilst language is a means to achieving those objectives. By means of visual clues, careful explanation, the use of cross-cultural analogies, collaborative learning strategies and additional support, emergent bilingual pupils can gain access to the curriculum, whilst unconsciously acquiring English. The Literacy Strategy, with its emphasis on word- and sentence-level work and learning strategies that involve shared and guided reading and writing, provides bilingual pupils with a framework for learning the structures of English.

Dulay, Krashen and Burt (1982) have represented the gradual process of additional language acquisition by means of a model known as the 'interlanguage continuum'. The interlanguage continuum is similar to the process of first language acquisition and represents phases in a learner's emergent competence of the target language. Utterances in a new language may be preceded by a silent period in which the learner listens to the target language. During this stage learners are 'tuning-in' to the rhythm and cadences of the language, as well as using visual clues to make sense of what is being said. Understanding of a language is usually in advance of an ability to speak it, and teachers can make assessments of emergent bilingual pupils by carefully watching their responses to instructions and explanations. In the early stages emergent bilingual children will take their cues from other children by watching what they do and by responding accordingly. One indication of the child's increasing understanding of English is represented by a decrease in their need to take visual cues from their peers or verbal prompts from pupils who speak their first language. Initial utterances in English are likely to be single words, usually nouns, followed by two- and three-word utterances, which can include structures that combine pronouns, verbs and nouns such as 'me/I want pen'. The latter stages of acquisition include such features as the overuse of the regular form of verbs to denote past time, e.g. 'I wented to the cinema.' It is a mistake to view these forms as errors and is more appropriate to see them as markers of the bilingual pupil's linguistic progress towards English. As such, they provide useful indicators for assessment purposes.

Supporting EAL acquisition through curriculum delivery

Whilst the classroom is the best place for additional language acquisition to occur, the bilingual child's rate of progress will depend on the appropriateness of the support provided. In the past, academic work for bilingual pupils has tended to be differentiated to the same level as for pupils who have a special educational need (SEN). Often bilingual pupils have been placed alongside SEN pupils in classes where children are grouped according to ability. Whilst some bilingual pupils will have a special educational need, which is likely to be in proportion to SEN pupils in the school population, around 20 per cent, it is essential that early formative assessments are made of bilingual pupils in order to judge the child's potential to learn. In the absence of standardised forms of bilingual assessment, such assessments are likely to be subjective. However, bilingual colleagues can provide monolingual teachers with an informed view of the child's first language competence and level of conceptual awareness. Such assessments can be used to place the child in an ability group that is more appropriate to their academic potential.

Once an approximate view of the child's ability has been made, appropriate forms of support can be devised. The conditions that make rapid acquisition of an additional language possible include;

- a stress-free learning environment;
- tasks that focus on curriculum access;
- scaffolded learning strategies;
- comprehensible language input;
- collaborative group work;
- supportive pupil networks;
- rich and varied contexts for talking and listening to English;
- an inclusive classroom ethos which incorporates linguistic and cultural diversity;
- opportunities to encounter new concepts through the medium of a first language;
- visual aids;
- explicit modelling of the structures of English.

The emphasis in the Literacy Strategy of study at word, sentence and text level enables teachers to model grammatical and textual structures of English. The effective use of shared and guided reading and writing should help to make the structures of different text types transparent for all pupils, including bilingual pupils.

Learning a new language is cognitively demanding in itself. Pupils who are in the early stages of acquiring English will need support strategies that enable them to access the curriculum and demonstrate understanding by means of tasks that are relatively language-free, or else are heavily supported. Given the point made above concerning the length of time it may take a bilingual pupil to acquire the necessary competence in an additional language for independent curriculum access, the nature of support will require careful modification over time. As the bilingual pupil's literacy skills in English develop the kind of directed activities related to texts (DARTs) suggested by Lunzer and Gardner (1979) provide the pupil with effective scaffolding to read for meaning. Examples of some of these activities are provided in Part Two.

Checklist for teachers of bilingual pupils

The following checklist reflects many of the points that arise out of the above discussion.

- Do you know how and when children use the languages in their linguistic repertoire?
- Do you encourage the maintenance and use of the child's first language?
- Do you include different languages in the classroom through such things as displays, dual-language books, bilingual storytelling?
- Do you give bilingual children opportunities to use their first language to access the curriculum and to demonstrate their understanding?
- Have you spoken to bilingual children in their first language?

- Are you aware of the process of additional language acquisition?
- Do you assess the child through the medium of their strongest language?
- If your classroom is grouped according to ability or children are setted, are bilingual pupils placed with pupils of a similar ability?
- Do you analyse the language content of lessons and support pupils so they are able to understand curriculum-related and idiomatic language?
- Do you analyse curriculum content for cultural allusions with which minority ethnic pupils may be unfamiliar and support their understanding by means of clear explanations and analogy?
- Do you modify the curriculum to take account of the cultural diversity of the classroom and society at large?
- Do you seek advice when you are unsure about how best to support bilingual pupils?
- Do you ensure bilingual learners have appropriate language support to access cognitively challenging work?

3 Collaborating with colleagues

Traditionally, teachers have tended to work alone in classrooms, but with increasing numbers of Teaching Assistants (TAs) in both primary and secondary schools the ability to work collaboratively with other adults in the classroom is likely to become a generic teaching skill. This point is signalled in revisions to the standards for Qualified Teacher Status (TTA 2002). Whilst many teachers are quite used to planning in teams, the delivery of the curriculum in the classroom is still very much under the control of the individual teacher. The new requirements imply that teachers will need to develop new working practices and protocols if real partnerships between colleagues are to become a reality. For those schools allocated additional human resources through the Ethnic Minority and Traveller Achievement Grant (EMTAG), the management and effective use of additional staff is essential to raising the achievement of minority ethnic pupils. However, there are few models of good practice available for colleagues to emulate. In early-years classrooms where the employment of nursery nurses alongside teachers is commonplace, working practices rarely utilise the skills and abilities of both 'partners'. Indeed, in his study of working relations within early-years contexts Yeomans (1989) describes relationships as a 'partnership of unequals', and Robins (1998) has gone even further to suggest that the expertise of nursery nurses is so marginalised they are the 'invisible professionals'. Given these findings, there is clearly a need for schools to devise strategies to maximise the effectiveness of collaborative work between adults in the classroom. In the final analysis effects will be measured by the extent to which the learning and achievement of pupils is enhanced.

Effective partnerships between colleagues, with the intention of improving pupils' access to the curriculum and raising levels of achievement, is an important feature of inclusive education. Given the time-limited nature of EMTAG funding it is imperative that schools do not waste time 'feeling their way' towards effective practice. The model of collaborative work in schools outlined in Figure 3.1 draws upon the model of partnership teaching suggested by Bourne and McPake (1991) and provides schools with a framework for developing effective practice. In addition, the materials to be found in *Partnership Teaching*, which includes video data of colleagues and pupils working collaboratively, provides schools wishing to embark on collaborative practices with some excellent exemplars. My adapted model includes the requirement to monitor pupils' progress and achievement and to target resources to raise the achievement of those minority ethnic pupils identified as under-achieving. Before describing my model, I think it important to share Bourne and McPake's definition of partnership teaching.

What is partnership teaching?

Partnership teaching involves the cooperation of class teachers and support teachers at all levels of the teaching cycle: the planning and preparation of lessons; the implementation of teaching strategies and methods; the monitoring, assessment and evaluation of learning and teaching. Central to the partnership are the needs of all pupils within the class and the attempt to devise learning strategies that meet those diverse needs. Effective partnerships involve mutual respect between colleagues, equal status in the classroom and a shared responsibility for pupils' learning and achievement. Colleagues may wish to alternate teaching roles to reflect their respective strengths in subject knowledge and pedagogy so that pupils see the two teachers taking both lead and support roles. These features might be described as cooperative teaching, but Bourne and McPake's model includes an additional dimension, which makes partnership distinct from purely cooperative teaching. The additional dimension involves the dissemination to colleagues across the school of the good practice identified within the classroom where the partnership has taken place. By sharing resources and innovations in teaching and learning strategies, as well as new forms of classroom management, such as collaborative group work, the partnership model is useful for staff development, not just for the two teachers involved in the partnership but for all staff in the school.

A framework for partnership

Although the focus for the partnership is action within the classroom, the partnership teaching cycle must be firmly located within a whole-school perspective. There needs to be agreement amongst staff about the targeting of additional human resources, otherwise resentment may occur and the ultimate benefits accruing from the partnership may be ignored in some quarters. For this reason the model combines a whole-school perspective with a classroom perspective. Research shows that strong leadership is a vital characteristic in the success of effective multi-ethnic schools (Blair and Bourne 1998). The success of the model is therefore likely to be influenced by the extent to which it is seen to be embedded within an institution's vision of equal opportunities. Whichever class is targeted, teachers working in partnership need to work with clear objectives and have a specific time-frame within which to achieve those objectives.

A model of collaborative work in schools

Monitor pupil achievement

Ofsted (1999) has proposed that schools systematically monitor the achievement of minority ethnic pupils following growing concern that four groups of pupils in particular, Bangladeshi, Pakistani, African Caribbean and Gypsy Traveller pupils, persistently under-achieve in our schools. Whilst it has also been shown that some of these groups in some schools and some LEAs are 'bucking' the national trend and that there are gender and social-class dimensions to achievement (Gillborn and Mirza

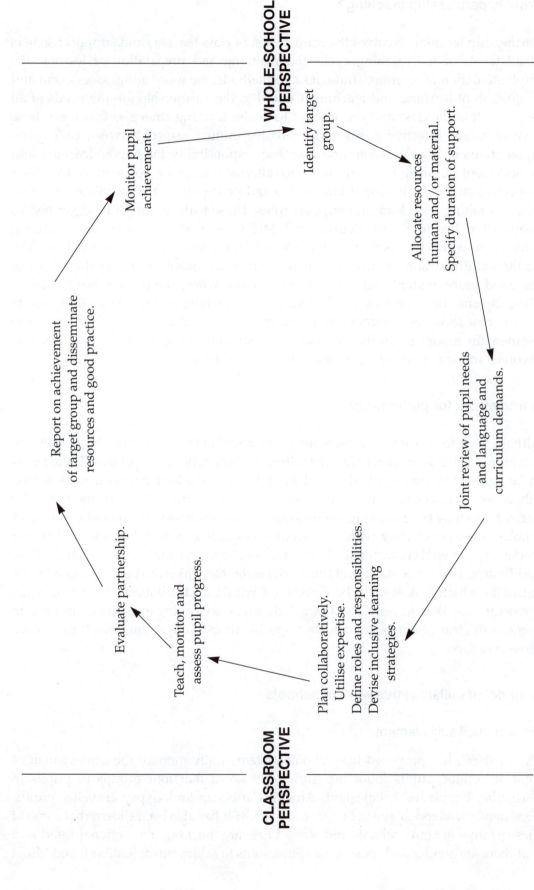

WHOLE-SCHOOL PERSPECTIVE

Identify target group.

Monitor pupil achievement.

Allocate resources human and/or material. Specify duration of support.

Report on achievement of target group and disseminate resources and good practice.

Joint review of pupil needs and language and curriculum demands.

Evaluate partnership.

Teach, monitor and assess pupil progress.

Plan collaboratively. Utilise expertise. Define roles and responsibilities. Devise inclusive learning strategies.

CLASSROOM PERSPECTIVE

Figure 3.1 A model of collaborative work in schools

2000), ethnic monitoring as a means of evaluating the extent to which equal opportunities are being realised is a key feature of a school's specific duty to meet the general requirements of the Race Relations (Amendment) Act 2000 (CRE 2001). The proposed model begins with the process of collecting data on pupil achievement. Such data can be collected from a variety of sources, such as SATs and QCA test results, reading ages and teacher assessments.

Identify target group

The second stage of the model involves the analysis of data in order to identify specific groups of minority ethnic pupils that are under-achieving relative to their peers in other ethnic groups. Once patterns have been identified, thought needs to be given to the underlying reasons for the under-achievement of particular groups of pupils. The process of identification is also likely to include consideration of how to effectively support, at school level, those pupils identified as most needy. Since the ultimate purpose of partnership teaching is to improve learners' access to the curriculum and raise levels of achievement, school assessment and monitoring systems need to efficiently identify those groups of pupils most likely to benefit from additional support. It may not necessarily be those pupils in acute need of English language support, such as newly arrived migrant pupils with little or no English, who become the target group. The school may wish to target a pupil cohort that is on the threshold of higher levels of achievement. In this respect the identification of the target group is likely to be influenced by overall targets set by the school.

Allocate resources

Due to the tight budgets of many schools, important decisions will need to be made about how to manage finite human and material resources. The exact targeting of resources is also likely to influence, and in turn be influenced by, curriculum organisation. For example, additional adult support could be allocated to boost levels of literacy within specific classes in a particular year group. Year teams could timetable literacy lessons to follow consecutively in several classes making it possible for an EMTAG teacher or a teaching assistant to support pupils who are working within the same programmes of study and learning objectives. In this way, partnership teaching could be established with several teachers simultaneously, particularly if planning takes place in teams. In secondary schools additional support might be targeted at particular year groups in a specific subject department. These kinds of arrangements are more likely to enable support staff to familiarise themselves with particular subject knowledge and to develop positive working relationships than if their support is spread thinly across several subjects and year groups. Careful judgements will also be needed when setting the duration of support and deadlines for assessment and evaluation of the partnership.

Review pupil needs

Before teachers can plan at the micro-level of the year group or class, it will be necessary for colleagues to jointly review pupil needs in relation to particular programmes of study, level descriptors and the linguistic and conceptual demands of the curriculum. The National Curriculum remains largely ethnocentric (Gardner 2001), which implies that a review of curriculum demand involves an analysis of its cultural 'load'. Part of the expertise of many EMTAG teachers and teaching assistants includes the ability to know when cultural allusions in the curriculum are likely to impede understanding. They are also adept at suggesting modifications that make the curriculum more inclusive of the languages and culture of the target group. Cognitive and social constructivist learning theories have highlighted the importance of building upon children's existing experience, understanding and conceptual formations. Through working within cultural frames of reference that are understandable to targeted pupils, lesson content can become an effective scaffold to learning. Detailed records of pupils' achievements and progress will ease the review process.

Plan collaboratively

Classroom or subject teachers and EMTAG colleagues are likely to approach the planning process from different perspectives. The 'mainstream' teacher's perspective is likely to focus on the subject content of the lesson whereas the EMTAG colleague's focus is more likely to be on the lesson's linguistic and cultural content. Utilising each other's knowledge and expertise in the process of joint lesson planning will fuse the two perspectives into a coherent whole. In addition to setting specific and achievable learning objectives, decisions about the structure and delivery of the lesson will focus on appropriate teaching strategies and the learning styles of pupils in the class. EMTAG colleagues grounded in the use of collaborative learning strategies such as those outlined in Part Two of this book can be influential in revolutionising the management and processes of learning. Equally important can be the use of a language other than English to enable bilingual pupils to access the conceptual context of the curriculum. Bilingual staff can obviously facilitate this, but so too can pupils if they are encouraged to work collaboratively in their first, or home, language.

Clearly, roles and responsibilities will need to be defined so that both adult partners have mutual awareness of each other's professional expectations in terms of the preparation of materials and resources, the delivery of different parts of the lesson, monitoring and formative assessment and the support of particular groups and individuals.

Teach, monitor and assess

One of the important features of partnership teaching is the sharing of teaching and assessment. Colleagues who have worked in this way often talk of how teaching is less stressful, how there is more opportunity to interact with pupils and really assess their thinking, and how it is possible, even during the course of the lesson, to share different views on what is happening. Having two colleagues in the classroom makes it possible for more pupils to be assessed in each lesson, which enables more up-to-date and comprehensive records to be kept.

Evaluate partnership

In addition to joint evaluations of teaching and learning at the end of each lesson, colleagues in the partnership will need to evaluate the overall effect of the partnership.

Amongst the factors to consider will be:

- the extent to which achievement has been raised;
- comparative levels of confidence and self-esteem amongst pupils before and after the partnership;
- how modifications to the curriculum influenced learning;
- the effect of bilingual support;
- the influence of particular teaching and learning strategies and classroom management techniques.

One other key factor to consider will be how the professional development of the colleagues involved was enhanced by the partnership.

Report achievement and disseminate

It is important that colleagues outside the immediate partnership have the opportunity to see the effect of collaborative work. Whilst statistical data can be presented at a staff meeting to show the quantitative effect on the target group's achievement caused by the partnership, feedback to staff on the processes and qualitative aspects of the arrangement are more appropriate to staff development days. Colleagues will then have the opportunity to explore and reflect on the detail of partnership teaching. The cascade effect of imparting good practice is also likely to be more effective if colleagues are given time to see how key findings from the partnership might enhance their own teaching. In this way the model of collaborative work in schools can be integral to the management of change for inclusive education. However, the process does not end with one partnership arrangement, because schools are expected to continually monitor pupil achievement. The identification of other cohorts of pupils in need of additional support will result in the formation of fresh partnerships, but ones that can build on the findings of previous partnerships. The model of collaborative work can be used by schools as a practical instrument to raise attainment and develop equality of opportunity.

4 Collaborative learning

The educational value of group work

Some educationalists have argued that group work leads to low-level thinking. This is perhaps because the research that led to such an assertion may have been based on poor quality group work in the first place. Indeed, although most primary classrooms appear to be organised for group work, research shows that rarely are pupils engaged in learning as groups (Galton *et al.* 1980; Galton *et al.* 1999). Ainscow (1999) also points out that active learning in groups is an under-utilised strategy and that its educational value is not widely realised by teachers. However, a small but growing body of teachers recognise the value of group work as a useful method in their repertoire of teaching and learning strategies. In particular, the pedagogy employed by many teachers funded through the Ethnic Minority and Traveller Achievement Grant (EMTAG) puts great stress on bilingual pupils talking with their monolingual peers in small groups, as a means of developing their English language skills. Indeed, educationalists working in the field of multicultural education have long advocated that well-prepared and well-structured group work is one means to achieving a more inclusive classroom. It is not enough for pupils to sit alongside one another in multicultural classrooms. This will not automatically lead to cross-cultural understanding. However, cooperative learning techniques, which rely upon interaction between peers in heterogeneous groups, are a proven means to improved inter-ethnic understanding and have long-term benefits (Coelho 1998: 140). Perhaps the single most ardent advocate of collaborative learning has been Stuart Scott, Director of the Collaborative Learning Project (see Directory of Organisations, p. 90). The project disseminates tried and tested, teacher-produced resources that facilitate structured, task-oriented group work. Drawing on research conducted in Britain and the USA, Corden (2000) has identified a number of educational benefits accruing from well-structured group work, in which pupils collaborate to accomplish shared learning goals. The various benefits of group work included:

- enhanced cognitive development;
- greater reflective and hypothetical thought, achieved through exploratory talk;
- greater scaffolding of pupils' comprehension skills;
- improvements in pupils' ability to make important connections between the processes of reading and writing;
- the stimulation of reading ability and critical thought;
- the development of metalinguistic awareness;
- improved motivation;

- more cooperative behaviour amongst pupils;
- the development of positive attitudes to learning;
- improved self-esteem;
- improved interpersonal and social skills;
- greater time spent by pupils on tasks;
- improved levels of educational achievement.

This is an impressive list of educational outcomes, which makes the under-use of group work even more remarkable. From my own experience, I have found that some teachers find the idea of collaborative learning a daunting prospect because they fear it will adversely affect pupil behaviour and their own classroom management. In practice, their fears have been unwarranted. On one occasion, I used a jigsaw activity (see p. 20) with a year group of about one hundred pupils. They were fully absorbed in the task and their focus on learning obviated any need for intervention on my part. Indeed, the session enabled me and my two colleagues to observe, monitor and assess progress in a way that is often more difficult with traditional forms of teaching. As this example suggests, one way of alleviating teachers' anxieties is by means of partnership teaching in which a colleague experienced in the techniques of collaborative learning works alongside a less experienced colleague in the classroom. With the advent of Advanced Skills Teachers and the deployment of EMTAG staff in schools, this is a real possibility, rather than a pipe dream. Colleagues engaging in such partnerships need to share in the planning and evaluation of teaching and learning, although the more experienced teacher may take the lead during the lesson. The inclusion of guided reading and writing tasks and group work in the Literacy Strategy, and the re-emphasis on learning objectives for speaking and listening, is likely to make collaborative group learning more widespread. Although group work has worthwhile benefits, as Corden (2000) and Alexander *et al.* (1992) point out, good education necessitates the careful match of appropriate teaching strategies to curriculum demands; the learning needs of pupils and classroom organisation. Group work is most effective when learning requires process-oriented tasks, such as discussion of issues, and the use of interpretive and evaluative skills.

Strategies for effective group work

Drawing on his work with the National Oracy Project, Roy Corden (2000: 99–103) has identified forms of collaborative group work that effectively achieve the educational outcomes listed above. The following seven strategies are summaries taken from his book.

Think–pair–share

Pupils are asked to consider an issue or problem on their own. They then join a partner and explain their thoughts. After this initial discussion, the pair join another pair to explore the issue further and arrive at a joint conclusion, which can then be fed back to the whole class. This approach lends itself to material that requires an evaluative response from learners or requires a group presentation.

Snowballing

This strategy begins with pupils working in pairs to discuss an issue or problem. The pair join another pair to share their findings. Depending on how familiar pupils are with working in medium to large groups, groups of four can be put together to form a group of eight and so on until a whole class plenary is reached. This approach is particularly useful when controversial subjects or material are being discussed and evaluated.

Rainbowing

Pupils begin by working on a common task in a group. Each member of the group is given a colour and new groups are formed based on the different colours allocated. In the new group pupils can compare findings and interpretations arrived at in their previous group. This strategy is a useful way to encourage pupils to question one another and justify their views, particularly if the original task called for critical understanding of a literary text. Corden also suggests this is a useful strategy for the drafting and redrafting of stories. Pupils work on each part of a story in one group and then join their colour group to share ideas and select options.

Dyads

Findings of the National Oracy Project suggest that pupils in Years R and 1 have difficulty working as a whole group. However, if the group is subdivided, so that pupils work in pairs on aspects of a subject, the pairs are then able to contribute information to the group.

Triads

Each pupil in a group of three is assigned the role of speaker, interviewer or scribe. The speaker begins explaining something they have learned about either through individual study, or during pair or group work. Using prompts and requests for clarification, the interviewer assists the speaker to fully explain their knowledge. Meanwhile, the scribe records the main points of the talk and reports back to the other two. This strategy helps to clarify understanding and thereby consolidate learning.

Envoys

As an alternative to having each group report back to the class at each plenary, envoys can be used. Each group identifies one person to go from group to group explaining and sharing ideas gathered from each group visited. In this way ideas and information can be disseminated relatively quickly.

Jigsaw

Corden comments that teachers in the National Oracy Project found this particular strategy very successful because it ensures that all members of the group are fully engaged in the activity. At the heart of the jigsaw strategy are three essential ingredients:

- A shared goal
- Individual targets
- Individual responsibility and accountability

Each member of a group is responsible for investigating a particular aspect subject. Pupils are then reorganised into 'expert' groups assigned with the same ar of investigation. In their 'expert' group, pupils assist one another to locate, under stand and identify the main points of information related to their subject. At the end of the investigation each 'expert' returns to the original group in order to share their newly acquired knowledge. When each group member has made their contribution the task is complete and the group has a fuller understanding of the subject.

A video of this strategy, as outlined by Corden, is included in *Partnership Teaching* (Bourne and McPake 1991, see 'The Life Cycle of the Salmon'). A variation of the jigsaw strategy that I have used is outlined below.

A variation on the jigsaw approach

Pupils are organised into small, mixed-ability groups. Each group is given an information sheet on a different aspect of a subject. Group members must cooperate to locate and record on separate answer sheets key pieces of information about their subject. At the end of this initial task each group has acquired specific knowledge about the subject under investigation. They are then referred to as 'experts'. The teacher then collects the information sheets. There are still questions about the subject pupils need to answer. To do this group members must elicit information from other 'experts' and take the knowledge back to the group so that all members can record answers on their individual sheets. It is important to tell pupils that their answer sheets must be left without the answers showing when they leave the group to gather fresh information. Pupils are forced to question, explain and clarify their understanding, which places great emphasis on collaborative talk. At the end of the session, when all pupils in each group have recorded the answers, the class is gathered together to check what learning has occurred. This approach has proven especially useful when introducing new units of work, but it could be equally effective for revision purposes. Some examples of jigsaw material I have used are on pp. 36–40.

The Brent Language Service (1999: 36–9) has identified other types of collaborative activity which enable bilingual pupils to move beyond 'social language' to more academic and curriculum-related forms of language.

From listening to writing

Pupils listen as the teacher reads a short text. On a second reading of the text pupils make individual notes of key words and phrases. Pupils then compare their notes in pairs, adding to them if necessary. Comparisons are made a second time but in groups of four with the end task for the group being the reconstitution of the text based on their notes. Reconstituted texts can be compared with the original version to note similarities and differences, during the plenary.

Objects to handle

Each group of pupils has a set of objects and a set of cards on which are written phrases, statements or quotations. The task might involve sorting the objects into groups of similar characteristics. Pupils then use the cards and a dictionary or thesaurus to describe each category. Alternatively, the objects might be ranked according to specific criteria or placed on a Venn diagram.

Brainstorming

Although this is a well-known strategy, which requires the quick-fire compilation of words and ideas, it has several secondary applications. The list can be used for ranking or sequencing activities. I have used a variation of this technique, which I call 'wordstorming'. Working in pairs, pupils either look at a picture or an object or listen to a piece of music. As they do so, on small pieces of card or paper, they list words and phrases evoked by the stimulus. In order to guide thinking and encourage observational skills pupils are asked to group words under specific headings such as 'colour', 'shape', 'texture', etc. If a thesaurus is introduced the number of words can be increased as pupils discover synonyms for words already listed. Pupils then pool their words to produce a piece of collaborative writing (see the example on pp. 48–50). By allowing bilingual pupils to record words and ideas in their home language an opportunity is provided for them to expand their vocabulary, where a word was previously not known in English.

Cloze and oral cloze procedure

Cloze procedure has been widely used as an individual reading activity, but the focus on word-level work in the Literacy Strategy makes it a useful strategy for shared reading with the whole class or with small groups. With certain key words omitted from the text readers have to use contextual, semantic or syntactic clues to find the missing word. The range of suggestions offered allows for discussion of appropriate words to use in the context depending on nuances of meaning. In pairs or small groups pupils could also use a thesaurus to find substitute words to replace those used by the author.

Barrier games

Individuals or pairs of pupils sit either side of a barrier. On one side is a picture which is described by the pupil(s) who have it in view. On the other side the pupil(s) listen and try to draw the picture as accurately as possible. Alternatives include the construction of an object, the completion of an incomplete flow-chart or map, the identification of specific differences in two similar pictures and following directions using similar maps.

Sequencing activities

Cut two different texts into their separate sentences, and shuffle them. Working in a group pupils have to first sort the sentences into two clusters and then sequence the sentences in the correct order. A more demanding version of this strategy involves pupils taking a 'hand', as in a card game. Each pupil reads their hand to the others, forcing them to listen carefully in order to arrange the sentences in the correct order. Similarly, a strip cartoon can be sequenced after each member of the group has described the 'frame' they have in their hand.

Homing in

Using a large picture containing numerous subjects, one pupil mentally selects one item. Other members of the group must identify or home in on the item by means of careful questioning.

Part Two

Strategies, resources and activities for language development and inclusive teaching and learning

5 Collaborative learning activities for Key Stages Two and Three

Introduction

Activities 1 and 2

The two literacy activities 'Big Brother' and 'The Chill Night Air' are designed for Key Stage Three pupils working with the Literacy Strategy, although similar activities could be devised for Key Stage Two. Each activity is divided into three sections, beginning with a cloze procedure, followed by several open-ended questions and ending with opportunities for extended work. Since its focus is word- and sentence-level work, the cloze procedure could be used for whole-class teaching, with or without the key words. The accompanying questions invite pupils to consider the text and its sub-textual possibilities. Unlike conventional comprehension work, the open-ended nature of the questions is designed to raise issues rather than lead pupils to find specific answers. In order to explore the sub-text, pupils need to draw upon their own experiences and knowledge of the world, especially their social and cultural awareness. For this reason, different pupils will have different interpretations of the text and will come to different conclusions, depending on their own social and cultural backgrounds, or knowledge of backgrounds different from their own. The questions should therefore elicit exploratory talk and will have a greater effect on learning if pupils discuss possible answers in pairs or small groups. The outcome of their group discussions and any issues and further questions that arise can be fed back to the whole class, which may lead to further discussion and sharing of knowledge. In this way, the whole class is involved and those pupils with particular cultural insights are likely to feel empowered. For example, in the case of 'Big Brother', pupils from Asian backgrounds may read the significance of Kamaldeep's presence differently from other pupils, although all pupils are likely to discern his possible disapproval of what he sees. Some may question why the older brother's name is Sikh whilst his sister's is Muslim. Does this imply that the brother and sister have parents of both religions, which would be unusual and could lead to discussion of further issues? How would the parents view a possible relationship between their daughter, Ashraz, and Paolo, if one should develop? Other pupils may draw comparisons between this short text and other texts, such as *Romeo and Juliet*, where two young people enter into a 'forbidden' love match. The second activity 'The Chill Night Air' is not so imbued with cultural allusion. Most pupils will appreciate the fear of walking alone along a dark street at night, although reactions may differ according to gender and 'race'. These differences would make interesting discussion points in themselves. They are certainly likely to elicit from pupils their anecdotal experiences. It may be possible to discern similar patterns in experience. For example, there might be a tendency for girls to say they would not walk alone at night. Some pupils may connect the setting of the text, Lancashire, with recent unrest involving White and Asian youths in Oldham and Burnley. By means of skilful handling of the subject matter this could enable the teacher to explore with pupils the causes and consequences of this particular social problem. By engaging with their social world, pupils could be guided to devise creative ways of resolving conflict.

Through discursive practice pupils can be guided to see the links between personal experience, cultural knowledge and the interrelationship of different texts, and the relationship between text and social reality. They can also come to learn that their views, opinions and interpretations are valid. In addition to whole-class discussion, other extension work might include improvisation or extended writing in which pupils pursue some of the sub-textual strands elicited during their group discussions.

Activity 3

'Refugee' is the opening to a story in which a family of refugees set sail in a small boat. Like the two previous activities, this one is also language-based, but like them the content demands cross-cultural understanding. The story is based on the 'boat people', who were Vietnamese refugees, but the setting is timeless, which leaves space for the reader to construct meanings that are unrestricted by a specific knowledge. Of course, there may be pupils reading this who are themselves refugees and who may interpret the text through the specificity of their particular experience.

This activity enables pupils to explore the relationship between written and visual images by encouraging reflective reading. It also draws on pupils' implicit visual literacy, gained through watching television and using newer forms of communication technology. Working in pairs, pupils first read the text. On a second reading, pupils need to think of themselves as prospective film directors who are going to turn the story into a film. They must decide how many shots the opening of the story will need and what will be in each shot. It is helpful if this activity is preceded by a viewing of a short film clip and an accompanying discussion in which attention is drawn to such things as how the camera was used to create different types of shot, including zooming in on a subject, close-ups, panning, etc. Pupils could be asked to share their experience of books they have read that have also been made into films and how the two differed.

As they read the text a second time pupils must decide how many shots the piece will need and identify each new shot by making an oblique in the text. Two 'screens' have been provided at the foot of the text, although more will be needed. On each screen, pupils draw the image that will appear. There should be one screen for each oblique made in the text. The strategy encourages pupils to scrutinise the text carefully and make constant reference to it in order to accurately reflect its content and meaning. During the plenary pupils can compare their respective screens, identify similarities and differences and give explanations for their choices. Again, this calls for close reference to the text.

The activity can be extended in the following ways:

- listing props or special requirements;
- identifying appropriate music;

- adding dialogue, commentary or narrative captions beneath each screen;
- continuing the story-board and then using each screen to extend the narrative.

Activity 4

This material tells the story of a short journey taken by Mai's grandfather as he walks across town to her house. It is her birthday and, en route, the grandfather searches for a present for his granddaughter. The task requires a pupil or pupils, working in pairs, to show understanding of written directions by colouring parts of a map in different colours, as directed by the text. Pair work can be advantageous if a fluent reader is paired with a less fluent reader. The cooperative nature of the task also generates talk between the two pupils, which is beneficial for the English language development of bilingual pupils.

Activity 5

The 'Introduction to Judaism' materials are designed to be used as a jigsaw activity. Each pupil has a copy of the grid sheet. There are six separate pieces of information. This particular activity could be organised for groups of six, in which case each pupil would have a separate information sheet. Individuals in the group would be required to share the knowledge they have gleaned from each sheet in order to answer all the questions on the grid sheet. Alternatively, the class could be organised into small groups with each group having a separate sheet. The group would be able to answer several questions on the grid sheet but would have to go to other groups, or individuals in other groups, to complete all the answers. See the fuller explanation of the jigsaw approach in Chapter 4, 'Collaborative learning'.

Activity 6

This activity includes eight character cards and a grid. Each card carries information about a character from Greek mythology. After reading the information, pupils complete a grid, which asks for specific information about each character. The task is best undertaken as a jigsaw activity. This would enable pupils to read the information and then share their findings orally, as well as record the information on the grid.

ACTIVITY 1: 'BIG BROTHER' (LITERACY KS3)

A small _____ of Year 11 boys _____ Ashraz as she walked down the corridor. Although she appeared to take no _____ of their intense admiration of her, she made her movements _____ slow and graceful. What she wasn't _____ of were the _____ eyes of her older brother, Kamaldeep, who watched the teenage drama from the _____ of the Sixth Form Common Room. Nor could she have _____ that he had seen the special _____ that Paolo Romana had paid her. When she reached the end of the _____, well out of _____ of the Common Room, she turned for the briefest of _____, caught Paolo's eye and gave him the tiniest _____ of a smile, before disappearing into the Drama Room.

known	seconds	doorway	deliberately	corridor	aware	
notice	sight	hint	attention	studied	group	suspicious

What do you think?

What might Kamaldeep be thinking when he sees the boys watching his younger sister?

What do you think of the way Ashraz reacted to being watched?

Why do you think the writer has referred to only one of the group of boys by name?

Do you think this is the first time Ashraz has noticed Paolo's attention to her?

What do you think Kamaldeep will do about what he has seen?

Do you think there is more to the situation than meets the eye?

If this story were developed what problems might be created for each of the characters? Who else might be involved and how might the story end?

ACTIVITY 2: 'THE CHILL NIGHT AIR' (LITERACY KS3)

The street was empty. Tiny pools of yellow light punctuated the _____ pavement along one side of the road. Aziz walked _____ towards his house at the far end of the street. The wind was sharp and he could feel _____ imminent bitterness in the chilly Lancashire air. Above him the moonless _____ was pierced by tiny pinpricks of silver _____. He paused for a moment, looking up at the _____, at the delicate pattern they made against the ebony _____ of the heavens. Compared to the vast night sky he felt very _____ and humble. Suddenly, from across the road, a hoarse _____ called out to him. Aziz was caught off _____. He turned to run, hesitated and turned, peering into the gloom. A _____ figure stepped out of a doorway. Aziz didn't _____ to find out who the man was or what he wanted.

voice	winter's	wait	dark	guard	light
briskly	sky	tall	small	stars	backcloth

What do you think?

What do you think about when you look at a clear starlit sky? Does it make you feel like Aziz did, small and humble?

What reasons might there be for Aziz walking briskly down the street?

Why do you think the writer described the night sky before the man shouted?

What would you do if someone called out to you whilst you walked alone along a dark empty street?

What evidence is there for Aziz feeling threatened?

What possible reasons might there be for the man calling out to Aziz?

Aziz didn't wait to find out what the man wanted, but consider the possible outcomes if he had waited. What might be the consequences of any one of those outcomes?

ACTIVITY 3: 'REFUGEE' (LITERACY KS3)

A cool breeze filled the mainsail, causing it to flap rhythmically like a limp bat's wing as the boat slid effortlessly through the still waters of the harbour. Set against the modern backdrop of marble white skyscrapers and the sharp, irregular horizon, the tiny boat seemed out of place and of another time.

In contrast to the frenzied populace of the mainland streets, the crew set about their long voyage ahead with calm determination. They had no worries about meeting deadlines. This journey would not be bound by schedules that harness the modern soul to the carriage of time. There was not a single clock or watch aboard. In this sense the journey would be timeless, and so it proved.

Further out the sea rippled and darkened. Tan Leung, who had been securing a loose rope, paused to look at the receding coastline; its office blocks and dwellings were now a brilliant blur surmounted by the verdant arc of the mountains. The small vessel began to roll gently with the swell and fall of the sea, causing Tan Leung to steady herself as she resumed preparations for the voyage.

On an old wooden packing case, at the other end of the deck, sitting motionless and staring blankly out to the widening sea was Tan Leung's grandmother. Through her grey, misty eyes distance was immeasurable; the horizon an imperceptible girdle. Conscious only of the gentle movements of the sea and the soft lulling sound of the water as it lapped the wooden hull, her thoughts drifted to distant shores, to a time when youth filled her now aching limbs with grace and elegance. She remembered, oh how she remembered, the sweet fragrance of the mimosa tree in full bloom, she recalled the long happy days spent in the company of the other women, the songs they sang and the stories they told as they worked in the shadow of the verandah. In the days before the soldiers came life had seemed a steady, simple existence.

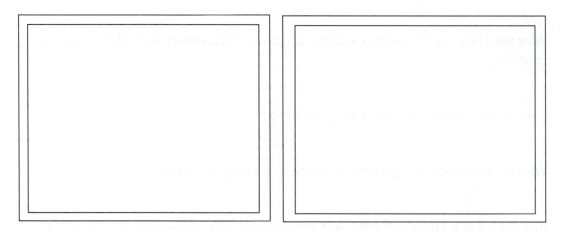

ACITIVITY 4: 'MAI'S BIRTHDAY' (BARRIER ACTIVITY KS2)

Mr Chan is going to visit his granddaughter, Mai. It is her birthday. Mai lives on the other side of town to Mr Chan. He does not have a car, and as it is a warm day Mr Chan decides to walk to Mai's house. Mr Chan leaves his house, which is next to the fish and chip shop in Church Street.

Find Mr Chan's house and colour it red. Tell me when you have finished.

Follow Mr Chan's journey on your map.

Mr Chan walks along Church Street and turns right. He then walks along Long Road to Avon Street, where he turns left. At the end of Avon Street is a garage. Opposite the garage is a pet shop. Mr Chan looks in the pet shop for a present for Mai.

Colour the pet shop green.

Inside the pet shop there are lots of cages. In some of the cages there are tiny birds, in the other cages there are baby rabbits. Mr Chan remembers that Mai does not like seeing animals in cages so he leaves the shop.

He walks to the High Road where he turns right. He crosses the High Road at the zebra crossing in front of the cake shop. 'What a good idea,' thinks Mr Chan. 'I'll buy Mai a cake'.

He asks the shop assistant for the biggest cake in the shop. It costs four pounds and ninety-nine pence. Mr Chan then discovers he has left all his money at home. The shop assistant tells Mr Chan there is a bank next to the shop.

Can you see the bank? Colour it yellow.

Mr Chan quickly goes to the bank to get some cash and returns to the shop to buy the cake.

When he has bought it, Mr Chan leaves the shop, walks along the High Road, past the garage and turns right into Cross Street. He crosses the road in front of the police station and walks to the end of Cross Street. At the corner he turns left and crosses the zebra crossing at the side of the hospital.

Behind the hospital is the King's Shopping Centre.

When you have found it, colour the King's Shopping Centre blue.

Mr Chan goes into the Shopping Centre to look for a present for Mai. But once again he cannot see a present Mai will like. On the other side of the Shopping Centre is an exit, which leads to Silver Street. Mr Chan goes through the door. Now he is in Silver Street. Mai's house is nearby but Mr Chan still has not bought a present for Mai. He looks up and down Silver Street. On the opposite side of the road are five shops. Mr Chan is standing opposite Cannon Street. To his right are the flower shop and the sweet shop.

Colour the sweet shop orange.

To his left are three shops. The shop on the left, nearest to Mr Chan, is a clothes shop. Next to the clothes shop is a toy shop and at the far end of the street is a garden shop.

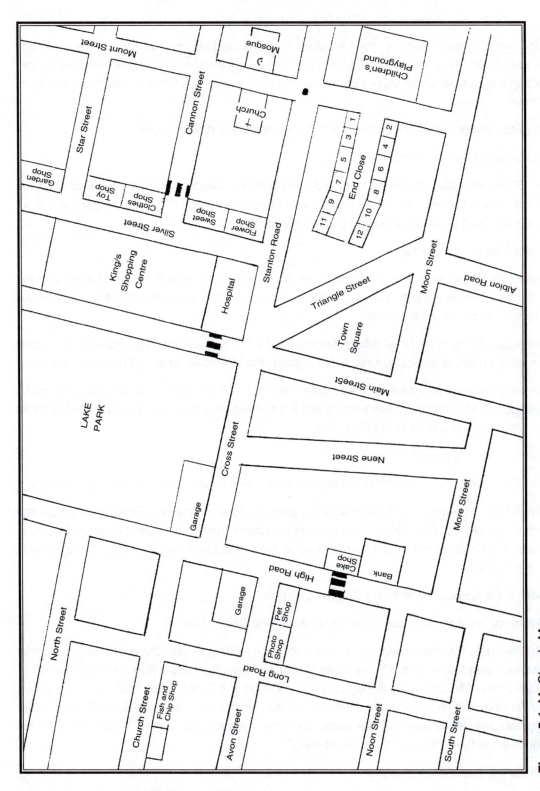

Figure 5.1 Mr Chan's Map

Write an X where Mr Chan is standing.

In the window of the toy shop is a bright red kite. It reminds Mr Chan of the kite he had when he was a boy. He decides to buy the kite for Mai and crosses the road. Mr Chan turns left when he leaves the toy shop and walks past the clothes shop. He turns into Cannon Street and then right into Mount Street. He passes the church, which is opposite the mosque.

Colour the mosque green.

Mr Chan continues along Mount Street until he reaches the children's playground. Opposite the playground is End Close, where Mai lives. Mr Chan crosses the road and walks down End Close until he comes to number 8.

Colour Mai's house red.

Mr Chan is very tired after the long walk, but when he sees his granddaughter at the window, smiling at him, he forgets about his aching legs. 'Happy Birthday, Mai.'

Extension tasks

After his visit to Mai, Mr Chan has to walk home. Give Mr Chan directions for the quickest route back to his house.

How many different routes can you find from Mr Chan's house to Mai's house?

ACTIVITY 5: INTRODUCTION TO JUDAISM (KS2)

Question grid

Where would you find a mezuzah?	When is Pesah?	Who was the first Jew?
What is Shabbat?	What is Succot?	What happens at Pesah or Passover?
When is Succot?	Which is the older religion: Judaism or Christianity?	What does Shabbat Shalom mean?
On which day of the week is Shabbat?	What is kosher?	When is Hanukkah?
What was the exodus?	When does Shabbat begin?	What is a hallah?
What is seder?	What is the Torah?	In which language is the Torah written?
Draw a menorah.		

Letter 1

10 Greendale Ave.
Walton Grove
Finchley
London.

20th January 2002

Dear Rashmi,

    Thank you for your letter. It was very interesting learning about the Muslim festival of Eid that comes at the end of the month of Ramadan. You wanted to know about our Jewish festivals. Well, I'm going to tell you about Hanukkah in this letter. Next time I write I'll tell you about Succot.

    Hanukkah was last month and is our festival of lights. It lasts for eight days. We have a special candle-holder called a menorah that holds nine candles. On the first night of Hanukkah one candle is lit, on the second night two are lit and so on until on the eighth night all the candles are lit. The middle candle is used to light the others. Hanukkah reminds us of a time long, long ago when the Jews were prevented from praying in the Temple in Jerusalem.

    Only after a ferocious battle, which the Jews won, were they able to go back into the Temple. The first thing they did was to light the lamp, but there was only enough oil for one day. By a miracle, the lamp burned for eight days, until more oil was found. That is why our Hanukkah menorah has one candle in the middle and eight branches to represent those eight days.

    Take care, Rashmi. I will write again soon and tell you about Succot.

Love,

Ruth.

Letter 2

10 Greendale Ave.
Walton Grove
Finchley
London.

1st February 2002

Dear Rashmi,

In my last letter I told you about Hanukkah and said that I would write again to tell you about another Jewish festival; the festival of Succot. Well, here goes – like Hanukkah, Succot also lasts for eight days. It takes place during the autumn and is something like the Harvest Festival which is celebrated by Christians.

Each year, at Succot, we build a little hut in the garden. From its walls and roof we hang fruit and flowers. If the weather is warm and dry enough we have a special meal inside the hut. Like Harvest, Succot is a time for thanking God for the food we eat. It also reminds us Jews of part of our history. After the Jews were led by Moses from slavery in Egypt, they lived for forty years in the desert. As you can imagine living in such a barren and infertile place was very difficult, but God looked after the Jews and saw to it that they did not starve. That is the reason we celebrate Succot and remember God's kindness.

Please write and tell me more about your Muslim festivals. I am sure that in some ways they are similar to our Jewish ones.

Lots of love,

Ruth.

Sam's diary

Thursday 19th January 2002.

Dear diary,

Today my friend John came to tea. Unlike me, John is not Jewish and at first he did not understand about things being kosher. After the meal he helped me do the washing up and kept mixing the spoons and pans. Mum explained about things being kosher. She told John that in our holy book, the Torah, there are rules which tell us what we are allowed to eat and how food should be prepared. John didn't know that cooking utensils used for diary products, like milk and butter, must be kept away from those we use to cook and prepare meat. Only when we obey the rules is our food kosher.

After that, John asked lots of questions about our home. As he left, he noticed the mezuzah hanging on the doorpost outside the front door. I told him that every Jewish home had one and that inside it are verses from the Torah. It is a reminder that we must never forget God. John asked if he could read the Torah but I told him it is written in Hebrew.

Next week I am going to John's house. I wonder what I will learn from him.

email: Nadia at Shabbat

Hi, my name is Nadia. I am Jewish. As a Jew I belong to a religion called Judaism. Tomorrow is a special day of the week for me and my family. We call it Shabbat and it is a holy day. Our holy book, the Torah, tells us how God worked for six days to create the world and blessed the seventh day.

At sunset the whole family sits together at the table to have a Shabbat meal. Mum says a prayer, 'Shabbat Shalom,' which means, 'Have a peaceful Sabbath.'

Dad says a blessing – 'the Kiddush' – over the hallah, our plaited bread. Shabbat is my favourite day of the week because all the family is together.

Information: Abraham

About 3,800 years ago there lived a man called Abraham. When Abraham was alive people worshipped many gods but he told them there was only one god, who created everything. God had told Abraham that his family would be a chosen people who were to be known as the Jews. So, it became that Abraham was the very first Jew. The religion of the Jews is called Judaism and the religion is older than both Christianity and Islam.

Abraham had a grandson called Jacob, or Israel. To this day the Jews are sometimes referred to as the Children of Israel and it was the name given to the land created for the Jewish people after the Holocaust, during the twentieth century.

One of Israel's twelve sons was called Judah. It is from his name that we get the word Jew. When the Jewish holy book, the Torah, was written all Jews spoke Hebrew. Today, Jewish children learn Hebrew so that they can read the Torah.

The Story of Pesah

It is spring again and we are cleaning the house ready for Pesah. We also call Pesah Passover and it is a very special time for Jews. Pesah lasts for seven or eight days. On the first day of Pesah we have the seder, a special meal.

Each thing on the seder table is a reminder of a story from Jewish history. The story of Pesah is over 3,000 years old.

Last year Uncle Jacob told us the story. These were his words:

> Now listen carefully. I am going to tell you a story from long ago; a story of when our people were slaves in Egypt. We had been slaves for over 200 years. Then Moses led us out of Egypt to freedom. Pesah is the story of that journey.
>
> God promised Moses he would help the Jews get their freedom. He told our people to mark their doorposts with the blood of a lamb. That night the angel of death was sent into Egypt. The angel entered every house and touched the eldest son in each family. That son never awoke from his sleep. Not one Jewish son died that night. Why? Because whenever the angel of death saw a doorpost smeared with the blood of a lamb it passed over the house. The next morning the Jews left Egypt. The long journey on which Moses took them is called the exodus. When they reached the Red Sea, the waters parted to let the Jews through. And so it was that the Jews finally became a free people once again.
>
> Now, every year the story of the exodus, or long journey, is told so we never forget that God gave us our freedom.

ACTIVITY 6: GREEK MYTHOLOGY (LITERACY KS2)

Characters

Heracles	*Odysseus*
I am an extremely strong and courageous man. I used to be very gentle. My teacher warned me what would happen if I ever drank wine, but I did not listen to his good advice. One night I drank too much and, in a fit of strength, killed my whole family. That is why I was sentenced to serve the mean King Eurystheus. He ordered me to complete twelve hard and difficult labours. I have finished them now and can rest, but I still regret drinking that glass of wine.	I am the king of Ithaca. I love to travel and have been on many a long adventure. One voyage lasted twenty years. Perhaps I was unkind to my wife, Penelope, by staying away so long. My cleverness has helped me escape many dangerous situations. I don't always believe what I am told. Like the time Circe told me not to listen to the Sirens. I was curious and wanted to know what the Sirens sounded like. Still, I am safe at home now.
Midas	*Theseus*
I am a king and a good friend of Pan. I was asked to judge a competition between Pan and Apollo, but I am a terrible judge and I let Pan win. Apollo was furious with me. For his revenge he gave me a pair of silly long ears like a donkey's. Then, when I had the chance to wish for something, instead of wishing the ears away, I asked for everything that I touched to turn to gold. Well, I got so carried away with everything turning into gold I could not stop myself. I did not learn my lesson until the day I touched my own son and turned him into a gold statue.	My father was the king of Athens, which makes me a prince. I am a very determined person, who never gives up on anything. I also hate cruelty and unfairness, which is the reason why I went to Crete to challenge King Minos and to seek out the Minotaur. I don't remember very much about what happened, though. Except people say I was very brave to do what I did. I wish I had a better memory. Even though I apparently showed great courage, I am also told I treated someone called Ariadne very badly.

Ariadne	Arachne
My father, King Minos, is the ruler of Crete. I am told I have a very kind nature but that I am not very pretty. I like to help people, that is why, when Prince Theseus came to slay the Minotaur, I helped him escape from the labyrinth. I did it because I hated my father's cruelty and because, from the moment I set eyes on him, I fell in love with Theseus. Perhaps I was foolish to believe him when he said he would marry me. At first, he took me away with him but then he abandoned me, alone, on an island.	I know that I am a very skilful weaver. Everyone was so impressed by my beautifully embroidered tapestries. They were the most wonderful creations in the whole world. Even the gods could not compare to my skill. I once said that I could even weave better than the goddess Athene. Unfortunately she heard what I said and challenged me to a competition. Afterwards, she accused me of being far too proud and boastful. I think she was jealous of my talent and that is why she turned me into a spider, able only to weave dull, grey webs.
Penelope	Persephone
For twenty years I waited patiently for my husband, Odysseus, to come home from his long travels. Even though there were many men who wanted to marry me, I showed no interest in them. In fact, I had to find clever ways to prevent any of them from marrying me. In the end, my love for Odysseus was rewarded when he eventually returned. At first I was not sure it was Odysseus, thinking he was just another man who wanted me for his wife. After twenty years Odysseus had changed, but he finally proved to me that he was my dear husband.	I am the daughter of the goddess Demeter. I love my mother very much and I love our beautiful sunny land of Sicily. When Pluto took me away to his cold, dark world under the ground, I was so homesick and sad. Pluto tricked me into eating some pomegranate seeds. I only ate them because I was so hungry. I had no idea that eating his food would mean I would not be able to return to my beloved land. But Zeus said that because I had only eaten six seeds I could live with my mother for six months of the year. The other six months, I have to stay in Pluto's dismal underworld.

Character	Who was I?	What did I do?	What kind of person was I?
Heracles			
Odysseus			
Midas			
Theseus			

Character	Who was I?	What did I do?	What kind of person was I?
Ariadne			
Arachne			
Penelope			
Persephone			

6 Collaborative learning projects

In this chapter I describe three projects that I have undertaken with pupils at Key Stages Two and Three. The projects combine whole-class, group and individual learning within a programme of work that promotes speaking and listening, reading and writing in an integrated way. The approaches to learning emphasised pupil interaction, the sharing of knowledge, ideas and experience and cooperation, in order to achieve learning goals. As has already been stated, collaborative learning provides a structured framework that fosters positive interaction between pupils. The use of collaborative strategies enables teachers to simultaneously cover certain cross-curricular dimensions and National Curriculum programmes of study. For example, the very nature of collaborative group work, with its focus on cooperative endeavour between pupils in order to achieve collective goals, emphasises the importance of developing pupils' social and emotional skills alongside other learning outcomes. Other aspects of spiritual, moral, social and cultural development (SMSC) may also occur, particularly in classrooms where there are children from several cultural backgrounds. In the course of collaborative work pupils tend to volunteer information about their culture that might otherwise be lost when using less interactive forms of learning. A by-product of the approach, then, is the 'multicultural capital' that pupils acquire through interaction with their peers who are from different cultural backgrounds. By multicultural capital I mean an ability to decode and understand the diverse cultural signs and symbols that exist in a multicultural society. Multicultural capital also involves a recognition that culture is not static, and that group and individual identities are equally diverse. Multicultural capital has been acquired when an individual feels comfortable with his or her own identity and feels neither inferior nor superior to people from other cultural, ethnic or racial groups (Gardner 2001: 29). Collaborative group work is one process by which learning can be made more inclusive but its full effectiveness will only become apparent if supported by a classroom ethos in which the sharing of knowledge is valued and acceptance of difference is the norm. Given this kind of ethos pupils are more likely to feel psychologically secure to take risks without fear of ridicule and rejection by their peers.

PROJECT 1: POETIC WRITING AND CREATIVE OBSERVATION

The teaching objectives for this project were:

- to build on pupils' existing linguistic knowledge;
- to work from objects that are immediately observable to deeper, more concentrated levels of observation;
- to scaffold pupils' writing by means of a systematic process beginning with word-level work and ending with the creation of coherent texts.

The type of scaffolding in this project involved the segmentation of learning into a sequence of short, manageable tasks. By developing control over each task, and by linking one task to the next, pupils are able to master complex tasks with a greater degree of control than if they had attempted them unaided (Gardner 1998: 14). Scaffolding is the pedagogic infrastructure that enables teachers to work with pupils within Vygotsky's Zone of Proximal Development (Vygotsky 1962). The ultimate purpose of the strategy I shall describe was to help pupils acquire a deeper understanding of poetic language and form, by exploring one process of how poetry is constructed. In so doing, the intention was for the poetic form to be demystified for pupils. The selection of objects can be oriented towards cross-cultural frames of reference, especially if pupils have encountered those objects in other curriculum areas and are able to bring a wider knowledge of them to the drafting process. An example of this is religious artefacts. When pupils understand the purpose and significance of particular artefacts in religious education lessons, they will be able to draw on that knowledge in literacy lessons. This cross-curricular influence is likely to lead to deeper and richer levels of thought and writing.

The drafting process

The work began with a whole-class activity. Pupils sat in a horseshoe formation on the carpet. In the centre was a *rehl* (pronounced rawal), a sandalwood stand used to support the Qur'an when being read. Although we had not looked at this object before, there were several Muslim pupils in the class and the sight of what to them was very familiar enabled them to share their knowledge. A positive classroom ethos in which pupils know that their contributions are listened to and valued, is an important feature of an inclusive multicultural classroom. The class was asked to look carefully at the object and give me words to describe its physical characteristics, such as colour, shape, texture, etc. I referred to this stage of the process as 'wordstorming'. Words were written on individual cards and were collated in lexical sets, i.e. under the headings colour, shape and so on. Once the wordstorm process had been exhausted and we had devised our word banks, I informed the class we were going to produce a piece of writing using only the words on view. Immediately some of them questioned whether this was possible, given the absence of such items as articles, conjunctions and prepositions. This suggested that they had begun to construct meanings because they were able to engage their syntactic knowledge and were implicitly moving between word- and text-level work.

We moved to the next stage after some assurances that we ought to experiment with the words and 'see what happened' when we tried to create a text out of them.

One pupil selected a word to start us off. A second pupil then chose a word that seemed to go with the first one. This continued until most of the words were used. At intervals, I asked the class if we should start a new line. We also paused several times to read the emerging text, which enabled us to move from the focus on words to a more global focus on the complete text and back again. This process of testing whether a word or sequence of words was appropriate within the textual semantic is essential to the development of compositional skills in literacy. Frank Smith (1994) explains that the development of writing involves the ability to move between focal and global aspects of composition, that is the writer's ability to alternate between a concern for a search for meaning within small units of text, a word, a phrase, clause or sentence, and the semantic of the text as a whole.

We then began to look more critically at our first draft by considering how the text might be improved. I suggested that if they wanted, the class could change the text by moving words from one place to another, or by omitting particular words altogether. Other changes could involve the relocation of whole lines or clusters of words. Individuals made their suggestions and automatically justified their reasons by using their ear for language with remarks like, 'it sounds better this way', or 'you wouldn't say it like that'. These comments enabled me to informally assess pupils' implicit knowledge of language. As with the initial draft we continually read and reread the text as it was redrafted. In doing so, I was scaffolding for pupils the process that experienced writers go through when they struggle to construct coherent texts. I think it essential that teachers should be writers themselves in order to understand that writing is not always an easy process, and to understand from the 'inside' what the process of composition involves. I was once surprised when I asked a group of 50 Primary B.Ed. students how many of them wrote, apart from their assignments. Very few did. In other curriculum subjects, students would be engaged in the processes they expect their prospective pupils to be involved with: in science they do experiments, in music they compose, in design technology they design and construct, so why not experience the process of writing in English?

After the final reading of our second or third draft, I asked the question, 'So what type of writing do you think we have made?' Several pupils said it sounded like a poem, which prompted a short discussion about the differences between poetry and prose. The pupils who had previously commented on the absence of prepositions and conjunctions etc. drew attention to the way many poems 'shortened everything'.

Following the modelling of the compositional process, which in National Literacy Strategy terms is an example of shared writing, pupils worked in pairs. Each pair had an object. In pairs they followed the same process to produce a piece of 'guided writing'. During the plenary some of the poems were read aloud. They were still in a 'raw' state, but it was clear the process had enabled pupils to write economically and sharpen their observational skills. Pupils were encouraged to say what they liked about the poems. They talked about such things as the quality of sound that was created by juxtaposing certain words and how the words created images in the mind. It was important to treat these embryonic works in the same way one would the writing of more experienced practitioners. Pupils responded positively to this treatment of their writing.

At the beginning of the second session I introduced the 'wordstorm' sheet (see below). Pupils were able to work more independently, but the sheet helped to

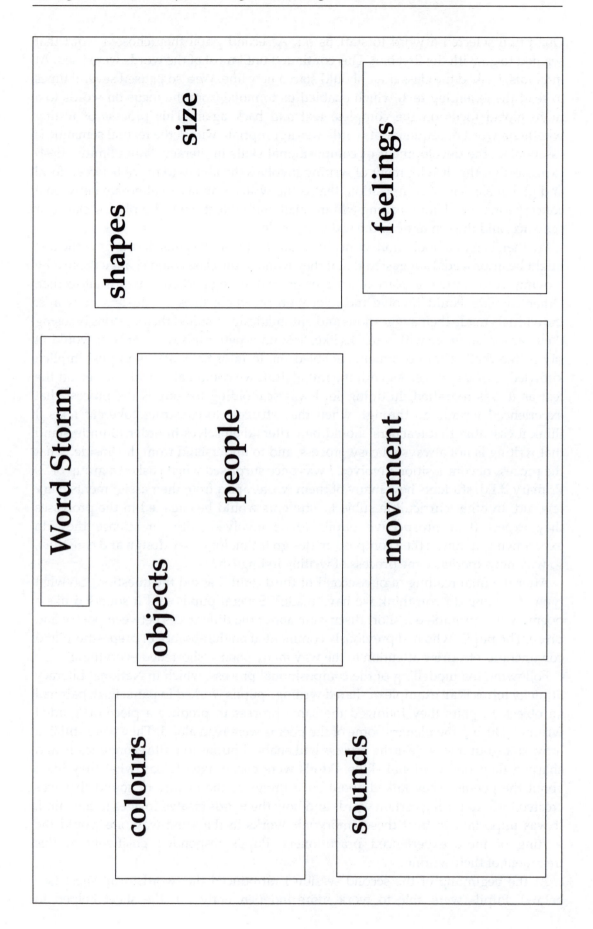

maintain a degree of scaffolding. Over several weeks other objects were introduced until quite mundane things became the subject for composition: an old glazed ceramic pot, a piece of dry sponge, a broken chair leg, a worn circular scourer. Pupils' responses demonstrated that they had become quite adept at evoking strong visual and aural images through language and at endowing quite ordinary objects with fresh insight.

This is how Aisha saw the scourer:

> Greenish, dark, multi-coloured.
> Circular, roundish, burger shape.
> Jagged, rough strands, hairy.
> Slightly small, medium.
> Scratchy, harsh, thin wiry
> Like a lid, spongy.

And Chris, an old piece of sponge:

> Smudgy black,
> Shoe shape
> Fairly big
> Soft
> Like hair
> Big lump of butter
> Yellow shades
> Rough and bumpy
> Medium size
> Fluffy
> Soft foam
> Like cheese.

I exploited the fact that some pupils were beginning to use simile in their writing by adding a section to the 'wordstorm' sheet which invited them to compare the object with something else. I added an additional stage between wordstorming and the initial draft. We read several types of poetry and talked briefly about what we liked in each poem. This strategy elicited poetry that was even more powerful and fuller in composition than the earlier work. Consider the lyric nature of Shahazan's poem based on a glass jar filled with tiny sea shells.

The Shell

> Sea shells cockle shells,
> In the roaring sea night falls,
> Out come the boys collecting
> Yellow, pink and orange ovals
> So come and collect with me
> Bumpy rough and smooth as a car bonnet
> If you want you can put them on a shelf
> To make it really nice.
> Glittery silvery shells glow in the night.
> Long fat big as my hand like rough stone
> Lime like a crime it's like a mantle

> If you put it near your ear it's like sea splashing.
> Oh no my mother's calling
> I think it's my bedtime.

Working with a painted mask from Indonesia, another pupil, Hafsa, evoked a terrifying impression, rich in aural imagery:

Hurricane

Without warning dragon of green,
The air twisting and turning as clouds come down,
As it cracks the ground as it moves
Sucking the air, as the sun hides behind the clouds,
You can hear the dragon hollering as it comes near.
It's whooshing around the mountain,
His teeth are rattling, 'UHT, UHT, UHT',
He bites through the mountain,
You can hear the cracks down the street
He is going bang, bang, bang, bang, bang.

At the end of the project, I collected all the pupils' poetry, including the poem we had constructed as a class, and produced a short anthology for each child to keep. We had a poetry reading and discussed the anthology. Then it was break-time. A number of pupils took their anthology into the playground. As I walked across the playground to the staffroom, it was gratifying to see pupils sharing their work with friends in other classes. These were quite 'streetwise' children, many of them from difficult social and domestic backgrounds, and for me it was one of those ecstatic moments in teaching, when you feel you have made a real difference. The pride in their work came from them and they were enjoying what they had achieved. This was a clear indication that the project had been a success. The quality of work produced by the pupils had shown that language learning had occurred, but what they did afterwards demonstrated that their self-esteem had improved too. We had begun with the spirit of cooperation, the sharing of ideas, and had ended with the pupils autonomously sharing their achievements.

Apart from the level of self-esteem gained by pupils through working on the poetry project, the process described above increased pupils' observational skills, their lexical knowledge, their understanding of how language can be structured in creative ways, and their feeling for the poetic form. Once pupils become natural users of poetic devices such as alliteration, assonance, onomatopoeia, simile and metaphor, and have a feel for the power of their own language-use, they are in a position to discuss and appreciate, at a far deeper level, the poetry of others from the vantage point of an informed insider. Fortunately, now that the National Literacy Strategy has become firmly embedded in the curriculum and there is renewed emphasis on objectives for speaking and listening and creativity, processes like the one described above can be utilised to tap the creative power that I believe resides in every child.

PROJECT 2: MIGRATION

The work outlined here has a direct relevance to parts of the Key Stage Two History Programmes of Study. In particular, the reference to the *impact of social and technological changes* in the study unit on 'Britain since 1930' refers to how immigration and emigration has changed local communities. The materials in this project include class and community surveys on the subject of migration. They create a meaningful context for learning by enabling pupils to explore the subject through the experiences of their own family and the families of other pupils in their class. The information provides real material for *data handling*, which can be represented by means of computer-generated software. Local patterns of migration could be compared to national statistics over time, which would provide pupils with the evidence to counter misinformation about immigration to Britain. Through discussion of key issues, it is possible for pupils to identify the underlying reasons for migration and the reason why many local communities integrate people from diverse social, cultural, religious and ethnic backgrounds. As a result, the work can lead to a greater understanding of the interrelatedness and interchange of societies and cultures, through the process of migration. In this way, the historical dimension of migration as a normal human activity can help to challenge parochial attitudes that equate ethnicity with nationality and territorialism. The project, therefore, involves cross-curricular learning, combining history, maths, ICT, English and citizenship, as well as aspects of social, moral, spiritual and cultural development.

The materials in this project include:

- Migration glossary
- Migration Survey 1
- Migration Survey 2
- 'People who have migrated'
- Migration chart
- Extension activities

Teacher's notes

Migration Surveys 1 and 2

Before embarking on the surveys with your class it is advisable to inform parents and carers about the project's underlying learning objectives. Parent or carer involvement will be imperative, since children will often need to ask members of their family relevant questions about family history.

'People who have migrated'

This activity and its accompanying Migration chart complement the local study by means of primary and secondary historical sources. To successfully complete this activity some pupils may need copies of a world map so they can check if a migrant crossed a national border and is an emigrant/immigrant. Copies of the Migration glossary would support pupils' understanding of subject-specific vocabulary. If conducted as a pair activity there is an opportunity for pupils to further develop their skills in speaking and listening.

Migration glossary

Migration

The word migration refers to the movement of people, animals and birds from one place to another. Many creatures in the bird and animal kingdom migrate quite long distances for part of the year. They usually do this because they need a warmer climate in winter or to breed. When people migrate they usually leave one place to live in another place. For example, if you were born in Newcastle and moved to live in Milton Keynes you would be a migrant. Milton Keynes is a new city and most of its population comes from people who have migrated there in the last 30 years.

Push and pull factors

People usually have good reasons for migrating from one place to another. There is rarely a single reason for them moving. Often there are reasons for leaving one place and other reasons for choosing to live in another place. These two sets of reasons are known as 'push' and 'pull' factors. A push factor is a reason for leaving the place in which you live. A pull factor is a reason for moving to a particular place. Some people have moved to Milton Keynes because there were plenty of jobs and houses there and have moved from other places because there was high unemployment.

Emigrate: to emigrate is to leave the country where you live to live in another country. This means you must cross one or more national borders to reach your new home.

Emigrant: when you leave your original country you are an emigrant. So, someone who leaves India to live somewhere else would be an emigrant of India.

Immigrant: When you arrive in your new country you are an immigrant. The word simply means that you have migrated from another country. So, someone who arrives from India to live in Britain is an Indian immigrant.

What do you think?

If you stay in your new country and have children will they be immigrants too?

The answer is no. They are not immigrants because they are in the country of their birth, they have not moved. It was the parents who moved.

Migration Survey 1

To find out about migration to the area in which you live, there are three simple questions that need to be asked.

- Where were you born?
- Where were your parents born?
- Where were your grandparents born?

Data collection

You could begin the survey by asking people in your class these questions, but you will need to give them time to ask their parents the same questions because not everybody in your class will know where their parents and grandparents were born.

Use the charts below to help you keep a tally of the answers.

Migration tally chart: class survey

The number of people in my class born in . . .		
	is	
	is	
	is	
	is	
	is	
	is	
	is	
	is	
	is	

Migration tally chart: survey of parents

The number of our parents born in . . .		
	is	
	is	
	is	
	is	
	is	
	is	
	is	
	is	
	is	

Migration tally chart: survey of grandparents

The number of grandparents born in . . .		
	is	
	is	
	is	
	is	
	is	
	is	
	is	
	is	
	is	

Now that you have collected the information, or data, think about how you could present it to other people in an interesting way.

Migration Survey 2

Why did they move?

People move from one place to another for a variety of reasons. Find out from members of your family that have moved and people that have come to live in your area, the reasons why they migrated.

Family survey

Members of the family who have migrated	Where did they move from?	Where did they move to?	The reasons why they migrated

Community survey

People in the local community who have migrated	Where did they move from?	The reasons why they migrated to this area

Push and pull factors

Now that you have found out why people in your family and local area have migrated, divide the reasons into two sets below.

Reasons why people wanted to leave	*Reasons why people were attracted to a new place*
These were push factors	*These were pull factors*

Sharing experience: What have people brought with them to their new home?

In a small group, list all the things you can think of that people take with them when they move from one place to another.

What evidence can you see in your local community of the contributions made to your area by the people who have moved from elsewhere?

People who have migrated

A

In 1963 the people of Kenya won their struggle to be free of British domination. Whilst the majority of Kenyans celebrated their independence, a minority of people who had British passports felt their lives were in danger. Amongst this minority was Harpreet, who has lived in Britain for over 30 years. She explains why her family moved here from Kenya.

> We believed there was no place for us in Kenya after Independence. Many of us were frightened. There had been a lot of violence in the struggle for Independence. We feared for our lives. Since we were British Citizens with British Passports, the natural place to come was Britain. We thought we could have a prosperous future here and, at the time, the British Government encouraged us to come because the country needed extra workers. Leaving Kenya wasn't easy though. I was born there and the country was full of memories for me. Even when the plane landed at Heathrow airport, I wondered if we had done the right thing.

B

The Irish have migrated to both Britain and the USA for many years now. Migration in larger numbers from Ireland began when the terrible famine of 1843–49 caused mass starvation. Young people in particular were tempted by talk of a better future and took the ferry to Liverpool, or sailed the Atlantic Ocean to America. Irish migrants in North America and Britain helped to build the railways. In Britain, they also helped construct the canal system. Today, the Irish community is one of the largest migrant groups in Britain.

C

Olaudah Equiano was born in 1745 in a village east of the Niger River, in what is now Nigeria. At the age of ten he was captured by slave traders and taken to the Southern States of America. The ship that transported him was overcrowded and disease spread like wildfire, killing many people. Imagine how frightened a ten-year-old boy must have been at being taken from his family and shipped to a strange land under the rule of an unkind people. Olaudah eventually gained his freedom and came to Britain, where he campaigned against slavery and social injustice.

D

Around the year 1500 BC, a group of people migrated from Eastern Europe, travelling across Iran and the Hindu Kush mountains to northern India. The Indo-Aryans, as they are now known, bred cattle. They needed fresh grasslands to feed the cattle, and it is believed this is the reason why they settled in the fertile plains of the Panjab.

E

After the Second World War and up to the late 1960s, many countries in Western Europe needed workers. There were not enough workers in these countries to fill all the jobs. The British Government decided to encourage people to migrate to Britain to fill the vacant jobs. Advertisements were put in newspapers in the Caribbean, India, Pakistan, Bangladesh and other countries. People in these countries had a long association with Britain, and many thousands of them responded to the advertisements, by moving to this country. When they arrived, however, they found that most of the jobs available to them were poorly paid. Even though many people felt they had been deceived, they could not afford the return journey home. They worked hard to make Britain their home.

F

The Industrial Revolution, which occurred in Britain in the late eighteenth century, caused a rapid movement of people from the countryside into towns and cities. Technological changes meant machines could do some of the work once done by people. There was less need for farmworkers, and the new machines in the factories could weave faster than people at home in country cottages. As life became more difficult for people in the countryside, they moved to the towns to find work in the factories. During the Industrial Revolution, roads, canals and, later, railways were built. This meant people and goods could be transported more easily.

G

> O, listen for a moment lads, and hear me tell my tale –
> How o'er the sea from England's shore I was compelled to sail.
> The jury says, 'He's guilty, Sir' and says the judge, says he –
> 'For life, Jim Jones, I'm sending you across the stormy sea;
> And take my tip before you ship to join the Iron-gam,
> Don't be too gay* at Botany Bay, or else you'll surely hang.

This is a verse from the ballad 'Jim Jones at Botany Bay'.

Botany Bay is a coastal area in New South Wales, Australia. In 1770 Captain Cook went there. Eighteen years later, the British set up a penal colony there. Convicted criminals were transported to the colony. Amongst them were people the Government didn't want, like trade unionists. The Tolpuddle Martyrs was a group of men transported to Botany Bay simply for forming a union to fight for better wages and working conditions.

---

* When this ballad was written the word 'gay' did not have the meaning it has today. The writer of the poem meant, don't be too joyous or happy. This shows that words can change their meaning over time.

Migration chart

	Who migrated	Push factors	Pull factors	Migrated from	Migrated to	Date of migration	Type of transport	Tick the boxes below			
								Crossed a border	Emigrant	Immigrant	Migrated voluntarily
A											
B											
C											
D											
E											
F											
G											

Extension activities

Using artefacts and pictures

An activity that I have found to increase pupils' confidence and self-esteem as well as their speaking and listening skills has centred on photographs and artefacts that children have brought from home. Pupils select a photograph or object that reminds them of the place they lived before moving to their present locality. Working in groups, pupils show the objects and photographs to one another and use them as an aide-memoire to talk about their memories of the place. By means of carefully constructed questions it is possible to elicit a range of knowledge from pupils, including social, historical and geographic information, as well as personal experience. Each group is then required to report to the whole class on what they have learned from each person in the group.

By talking about their past, pupils learn about one another and about themselves. The fact that their past is a valid part of the curriculum enables schools to implicitly show pupils that their experiences and identities are valued. In this way, the activity supports an inclusive ethos since it contributes to a positive 'hidden curriculum' as well as the overt curriculum.

Further work can involve research and displays. Library sources and the Internet could be used to find out more about places referred to by pupils. An interesting interactive display, using the photographs and artefacts in conjunction with regional, national and world maps to show the geographic location of places, would reinforce the importance of pupils' experiences. It is also likely that aspects of the work will have relevance to other parts of the planned curriculum, enabling the teacher to make explicit references to pupils' experiences. This will further reinforce the importance of those experiences and provide a means by which the curriculum can be related to the real world.

Language awareness

Pupils who originated in other parts of Britain and the world are likely to have a knowledge of varieties of English and languages other than English that may not be widely spoken in the locality of the school. Their knowledge of dialect words and variations in English syntax could be the starting point for a study of linguistic diversity. English is an eclectic language. Throughout its history, it has incorporated loan words from numerous other languages, including Chinese and Hindi as well as various European languages. One resource designed to explore the lexical roots of the English language is 'The Word House'. Each brick of the house has a commonly used 'English' word. The words originate from eight 'word families'. The words in each 'family' are displayed on a family word card. Family cards include languages such as Italian, French, Latin, Greek, Dutch and the aforementioned Hindi. Each card is a different colour. Pupils identify the root of each word on the house by colouring the bricks in the colour that corresponds with that word's family card. The end product is a multicoloured house that serves as a visual reminder of how other languages have contributed to make the English language so diverse and lexically flexible.

Did you know that the word for pineapple is the same in French, Panjabi, German, Greek and Danish? I discovered this when a German friend asked for *ananas* in a bar in Hanover. My wife, who speaks Panjabi, instantly understood his request. I have since discovered the word is common to the other languages mentioned. Pupils are often as intrigued as I was when they become 'language detectives' and investigate similarities between different languages. One possible starting point is similarities between French and English, where the difference between certain words is a matter of pronunciation, but lexical similarities occur in other languages too. An example is the word in Urdu, Hindi and Panjabi for tea, *char*. The word has been borrowed by the English language and many older English people will be familiar with the title 'char lady', the woman who served the tea in a café or factory. The Greek word for tea is similar, *chi* (long vowel). Equally similar are the French and Panjabi words for an upper garment, which are *chemise* and *kameez* respectively. A useful stimulus for younger pupils is the book *Grannies and Grandads*, published by A. and C. Black, which involves a class of pupils comparing the names they call their grandparents. Amongst the examples are Bapuji, Vanaji and, for English speakers, the more familiar Gramps. Towards the end of the book the various names are displayed on mobiles hanging from the ceiling of the children's classroom. Showing recognition of children's languages as a curriculum resource and representing them in the classroom is a further example of how culture and identity is valued in the inclusive classroom.

Drama and creative writing

In drama personal and social tensions can be explored through role play and improvisation; the causes of emotional conflict can be comprehended and reflected upon. The process of getting pupils to simulate real life situations and then analyse them can lead to real empathy and maturity of thought. The theme of migration lends itself to those tensions associated with leaving a place for good to live somewhere else. In some classrooms some pupils will have experience of leaving a place they have loved; in other classrooms perhaps the majority of pupils will have migrated. In a few classrooms there will be pupils for whom continual movement is a way of life. For each of these pupils there is a story to tell, and drama provides them with the means to share not only their experiences but also the feelings associated with those experiences. And for those pupils who have only ever lived in one place there is the opportunity to project themselves beyond their own situation and just for a moment to stand in someone else's shoes. In order to help create an authentic emotional setting for the drama we might ask a series of questions, including:

Who or what would you or did you miss most?
What might be or what were your last words and to whom?
How would you or did you say your goodbyes? Face to face, by phone, in a letter?
How would you or did you feel about leaving?
What would you or did you choose to take with you?
What thoughts might you have or did you have about the next place to live?

We must never forget that for a minority of children, particularly asylum seekers and refugees, leaving home could have been tragic and traumatic. Drama may be one way of enabling such pupils to better come to terms with their experience by giving them a voice. However, teachers will need to be sensitive to the needs of these pupils and be prepared to allow sufficient time to support them in appropriate ways.

An alternative to drama or an adjunct to it is writing. On a plain sheet of A3 paper, pairs or small groups of pupils write each of the above questions so that they are evenly spaced on the paper. Using the brainstorm strategy they then devise up to six possible answers and write them around each of the questions. The group then reflects upon the answers and selects the ones that seem most plausible. Ultimately the group will have one answer for each question and use these to help shape their writing, which might be in the form of a narrative, diary or autobiography.

Art

The architecture and variety of people in the local community can provide a rich source of visual stimuli for pupils. Classroom-based work on migration, which makes pupils more sensitive to diversity, can be followed by a walk around the local area to identify examples of diversity within the community. On their journey pupils sketch people and places that interest them. Back in class, their observations can be represented with greater care. By means of careful collaboration, their visual representations can be collated to create a colourful mural of the local community, which also stands as an important social document. Producing a class mural is a further example of how the process of collaboration can be used to help create a sense of class unity and togetherness. The subject matter for the mural, based as it is on the local physical and social environment, extends this sense of group identity from the class to the local community and encourages pupils to gain a shared vision of their social world. I recall one mural on display in a class of ten-year-olds depicting such images as a man wearing dreadlocks pushing a child in a buggy; next to him was a sign for the disabled toilet and a ramp leading up to it. By carefully integrating close observation and representation of the local community in their artwork with questions that encourage analysis, teachers can sensitise pupils to the positive features of social reality, and in so doing draw upon examples from the real world that challenge gender and racial stereotypes. The fact that the 'real world' referred to in this activity is within the children's immediate experience helps to dissolve the boundary between school and community and thereby reinforces both the notion that children's own experience is relevant to learning in the classroom and that learning takes place inside and outside school. Good teaching encourages multidimensional learning. Whilst encouraging observational, artistic and analytic skills, this project also provides the means for developing spiritual, moral, social and cultural awareness.

Geography

With knowledge gained about people and their diverse needs, and having carefully observed the local physical environment work, a further extension activity involves pupils planning a new community for a similar collection of people. Although ostensibly pupils are designing the physical layout of buildings and infrastructure, the activity requires them to apply the social and cultural knowledge they have acquired through their work on migration. Thought will need to be given to such things as the kind of residential accommodation required for different types of family, ranging from the single-parent family to larger extended families. Pupils will need to consider the most appropriate location of public services and utilities for the people who need them most, such as older people, disabled people, people without independent means of transport and families with small children. The inclusion of places of worship, such as mosque, church, chapel, gurudwara, mandeer or synagogue, can reflect religious diversity. People's need for work and leisure can also be included. Undoubtedly, pupils will be applying the knowledge of what they have actually observed in their locality and replicating it in their own plans, but they will also realise what is not there and what ought to be included, based upon a consideration of the needs of different groups of people within the community. Whilst the main objective for learning is the interrelationship of human and physical geography, the work helps to reinforce and consolidate awareness of diversity, multiculturalism and the importance of taking into account everyone's needs when planning for the future. If pupils have had the opportunity to develop this kind of theoretical framework in the classroom, they are more likely to carry it through to adult life and apply it as generalised perspectives in their vocational and civic life. In this way, long-lasting and important aspects of citizenship education run parallel with key learning objectives from other curriculum subjects.

PROJECT 3: NAMES

Chapter 5 of *Teaching and Learning in Multicultural Classrooms* (Gardner 2001) began with the sentence, 'For some children school can be a frightening place.' I went on to describe the effect that racist name-calling within school and the local community had had on a group of British Bangladeshi pupils. Over time, the persistent barrage of racial abuse, through name-calling and physical harassment, alienated these pupils to the point where a physical response was the ultimate means of challenging the bullies. A failure by the adult community to deal with racial abuse early on left both White pupils and their Asian peers with no alternative means of resolving the problems they had. This failure meant that both groups of pupils, in effect, were excluded from the benefits of living in a multi-ethnic society. For one group, their positive identity and very presence in the community was under attack; for the other, their ability to develop the necessary social and interpersonal skills required for inter-cultural understanding was denied. Inclusive communities and inclusive schools generate confidence and positive collective and individual identities. They are places where children feel both physically and psychologically safe. In order to reach this state of equilibrium, schools often work very hard to generate a positive ethos. Some of the groups listed in the Directory of Organisations (p. 89), such as Mediation UK, specialise in conflict resolution and offer advice to schools on useful strategies to help develop cooperative school environments. The project outlined below was under-taken with Years 6 and 7 in seven schools in one Local Education Authority in the South Midlands. Pupils spent one session a week for four weeks working with me on issues related to names and name-calling. I used a variety of techniques and strategies including circle-time, group work, drama, discussion, silent-reflection and writing to achieve the project's learning outcomes, which included:

- The ability to talk confidently about sensitive issues.
- The ability to empathise with the victims of bullying.
- An understanding of the effects of name-calling and bullying on both the victim and the bully.
- The identification of the reason why children bully.
- An understanding of what can happen when nation states become the ultimate bully.
- The recognition that individuals and groups have the power to challenge bullying and achieve positive relations in school.

At the end of each session, I collected pupils' responses and collated them so that the next session began with a report back of their responses. In this way, continuity of thought was achieved despite the gap of seven days between each session. What follows below is an outline of each session, together with a selection of the responses collated.

Session One

For most of this first session I used a circle-time approach. The circle is a very egalitarian shape since everyone is sitting on the floor at the same level, equidistant from the centre. By also sitting in the circle, the adult leading the session makes a positive, albeit perhaps subliminal, statement about being on the same level as pupils. The symbolic message is, 'everyone is included here, no-one is to be left out'. These symbolic signals are part of what has been termed the 'hidden-curriculum' and are important in establishing an inclusive classroom ethos in which everyone feels accepted, respected and valued. After a brief comment about having an interest in names and people's feelings about their own names, I asked pupils to stay sitting in the circle but to work in pairs and tell one another two things:

- their full name;
- why they were given each part of their name.

Each pupil then introduced their partner to the rest of the circle by telling them what they had learned about the other's name. Sometimes there was an even number of people in the circle, which meant that I was introduced to the class by one of their peers. On other occasions I had to introduce myself. The contribution of the adult leading the session is another signal to reinforce the twin concepts of equality and inclusion. Two supplementary questions followed, which also were discussed in pairs. These were:

- What do you like about your name?
- What do you dislike about your name?

This time, individuals gave their own feedback. After my own contribution and after listening to everyone else I gave a brief summary of key points emerging from the group. This enabled me to implicitly make another important point: that all contributions were valued and that we were all learning together.

Until this point in the session, I had asked pupils to share their thoughts in pairs before contributing to the whole group. This is because people often find talk less threatening in pairs and small groups than in large groups. It also enabled every pupil to be involved from the outset – another important aspect of inclusion. In fact, I often use the strategy of paired talk at the beginning of lessons for that reason. It also means the teacher can ask an important question about a subject, get everyone involved in thinking about the issue, ask the question again and get a good response from everyone in the class instead of a few keen 'hands' eager to share their knowledge. I have found this approach gets the lesson off to a really positive start because it engages the minds and language of all children in the act of focusing on a key issue. They are interested because they have been given time to become engaged in the lesson.

After each of the next three questions, I passed a soft object around the circle. As is the convention with circle-time, possession of the object gives the holder the right to speak if he or she wants to. This is another important strategy in the process of establishing an inclusive classroom because it gives every person in the circle the opportunity and time to have their say. The three questions were:

- If you were asked why is your name important to you, what would you say?
- If you have a nickname and someone who is not a member of your family or a friend calls you that name, how does it make you feel?
- If you have ever been called a name that made you feel angry or sad, who called you that name and what did you do about it?

In view of the fact that these last questions can lead to accusations being made about named people in the class or school, it is important to stress that the name-caller is not named, because right now we are interested in what happened and how individuals can sometimes respond to being called names, not in who did it. This helps to make the session more objective.

The final part of the session involved pupils working individually to record aspects of their own talk and thinking during the session. Not only did this give pupils an opportunity to record their talk, it also gave those who had chosen not to respond orally to the last three questions the chance to share their thinking on paper (see the record sheet headed 'Sticks and Stones', p. 69). I also asked the pupils to write their responses to the popular saying, 'Sticks and stones may break my bones but names will never hurt me.'

Examples of pupils' responses from Session One

Why were you given each part of your name?

- I got my first name, Georgina, because my granddad was called George.
- I was named after the title of a song.
- My first name is my grandmother's name. My second is my dad's surname. Part of my name means 'girl'.
- Because my ancestors were Welsh, I was given a Welsh name.
- I was given the name Gemma because my brother brought back a gemstone from holiday.
- I think my mum was reading a Lewis Carrol book, so she called me Lewis.
- Mayli Lim because it means beautiful.
- Because it means 'a gift from God'.

Responses such as these demonstrate the familial and religious significance of certain names. With awareness raised, the context is set for explanations of how different ethnic groups name newly born children.

What do you like about your name?
Pupils said they liked their name because:

- My friends use it to be friendly.
- Everyone else likes it and no-one makes fun of it.
- My parents gave it to me.
- It is unique.
- It comes from my parents' country.

What do you dislike about your name?
Pupils said they disliked their name when:

- Other people ridicule it.
- People distort it or make it sound rude.
- It sounds old-fashioned.
- People mispronounce or misspell it.

Answers to these two questions demonstrate how pupils' feelings about their name can be heavily influenced by other people's responses to it.

If you were asked why your name is important to you, what would you say?
Pupils thought their name was important because:

- It identifies me and no-one else in the class has my name.
- If I didn't have a name I would be called after my appearance.
- Without a name I would be called anything by anybody.
- It was given me by my parents who chose it after thought and discussion.
- It singles me out as an individual.
- Nobody would know who you are. My name is like my own trade mark.

As this final comment suggests many pupils had a clear sense of how one's personal name acted as a marker for their own identity.

If you have a nickname and someone who is not a member of your family or a friend calls you that name, how does it make you feel?
Pupils expressed a variety of different responses, including:

- I might feel annoyed, depending on how they said it.
- Angry and sad.
- Helpless to do anything about it.
- Don't care.
- Sometimes get annoyed when people say it in a horrible tone of voice.
- Most of them I don't mind but two I don't like.
- It makes me feel a bit silly if people who call me by my nickname aren't my special friends.
- I don't like people who are not in my family to call me by my nickname.

From these responses pupils began to realise how sensitive names can be, depending on who is using them and how they are being used. Nicknames are usually terms of affection that link the individual to important people in their lives. As far as their use is concerned, there is clearly an in-group and an out-group.

If you have ever been called a name that made you feel angry or sad, who called you that name and what did you do about it?

- When I get called a name I get very angry but feel hurt. I usually try to ignore it but have been known to react violently.
- I have been called fat many a time by a number of boys. It makes me feel hurt inside.
- I have had the micky taken out of me because of the colour of my skin. I tell them to get lost and just walk away.
- When I first got my glasses, in infant school, a boy called me four-eyes. This made me feel hurt but I just turned my back and walked off with my friends.
- I don't like it but I don't do anything about it.
- I wanted to hurt him but I didn't.
- I was annoyed at the time and when I got into the classroom I cried.
- I was once called a racist name by a couple of teenage boys. I was too hurt to do anything about it. I do not like to tell anyone about it.

- I told my dad because it was a racist name.

As this small selection of responses shows children often respond to offensive name-calling by 'putting-up or shutting-up'. Very rarely do they share their hurt with adults. Where name-calling is persistent, it is easy to see how keeping that continual hurt inside can be emotionally damaging to a child.

'Sticks and stones may break my bones but . . .'

I asked different groups to write in different ways about the saying, 'Sticks and stones may break my bones but names will never hurt me.' Some groups were asked to make a statement about the saying:

- I think it's false, names can hurt your inner-self and they could be harmful.
- I do not think the saying is true because you can get rid of physical pain by taking an aspirin, but you can't take a tablet to get rid of inner pain.
- Physical pain can go away in minutes but the pain inside can go on for weeks or months.
- Physical pain heals quicker than a name which can hollow your inside for days.
- Names can hurt you. It depends very much on what they are. For example, I often get called a swear word but that does not harm me because it's not something to do with me whereas if I were brown and somebody called me Paki it would hurt very much.

Other groups wrote a poetic response to the saying.

> Sometimes names can hurt; sometimes they can't,
> Sometimes you can shrug them off
> Sometimes you can't
> Sometimes they really, really hurt
> People deep down inside
> And for others it just bounces away.
>
> Sad and hurtful
> Tormenting
> I feel lonely
> Curled up inside
> Kicking somebody
> Some people
>
> Always so bitchy
> Nasty and unthoughtful
> Determined to hurt you
>
> Say sorry and it will be over
> Turn away
> Over and over
> Names can hurt
> Everybody
> So, just leave it out.
>
> Stupid and cruel
> That's what names are

Sticks and Stones

If you were asked why your name is important to you, what would you say?

Do you have a nickname?
(If other people, who are not your friends or family, call you that name, how does it make you feel?)

Have you ever been called a name that made you feel angry or sad? If so, who called you the name and what did you do after being called the name?

Write your full name in the space below

Why were you given each part of your name?

What do you like about your name?

What do you dislike about your name?

Hurting
Deep down inside
The people who say them
Won't know what it's like
They never think or worry for what that person is feeling
It's like being cut in two
That's what names can do to you.

Names, names, who needs them
Nicknames
Spiteful names
You could do without them
Slag, slut, whore, bitch,
Titchy dick, wanker, dickhead,
Boys and girls get them and dish them out
But when they come back,
Have you really thought about
What you are saying?

These are sensitive, personal and intelligent responses that show a deep sense of empathy. They are embedded in children's direct experience and draw on their social and emotional world. Some of them, particularly the last one, demonstrate the harsh and often sexist language that is part of playground culture. I found this to be a feature of every school playground irrespective of the social or cultural context of the school. The same comment applies to the use of racist language. The same words were occurring with the same frequency across all the schools in the project, which demonstrates the pervasiveness of racist and sexist language in children's oral culture. Whilst this finding is replicated elsewhere, it is also evident that children often have contradictory attitudes to 'race' (Troyna and Hatcher 1992; Gaine 1995). As teachers we therefore need to know what is being said and how pupils are responding to it before we can devise effective strategies for dealing with offensive names. What is evident from the responses of pupils in the project is that given the right opportunities children can be very articulate about the problems they encounter. By building on their insights, it is possible to construct collective solutions to what they all feel to be wrong and unjust about their social world.

Session Two

Taking this last point forward it was important that pupils received feedback on their responses to show that what they had written individually was part of their collective thinking. The feeling of being hurt when called an offensive name was common to most of them, but because it is something that they did not talk about, they were unable to find collective solutions to the problem. The first step in solving any problem is recognising the problem exists in the first place.

I began the second session with pupils sat in a semi-circle in front of me. After giving the feedback, I showed them a picture of a girl holding a cage. Inside the cage was a dead gerbil. The girl had a single tear rolling down her cheek. I used the picture to construct a scenario with the pupils. We gave the girl and her dead pet names and developed a brief narrative around how the girl was given the pet and by whom. I wanted pupils to explore, through drama, the way in which bullies victimise others. Working in small groups pupils improvised a scenario in which the girl arrives at school and tells her best friend about the gerbil. As she does so, the class bully overhears. The bully and a small gang of hangers-on later confront the girl and torment her over the death of the gerbil. We demonstrated the relationship of the girl to the bully during this second improvisation by freezing the action. The group 'statues' depicted the imbalance of power between the bully and the girl in a physical way, which enabled all pupils to see that the bully was only successful by making the girl feel weak. I then gave pupils a minute to write a statement about the reasons why bullies call people names. The following responses were typical of what most pupils wrote:

- Bullies call names to make themselves feel big and tough and to make you feel small and hurt inside.
- To make you feel useless and angry.
- To make you feel upset and like an outsider.
- To make themselves look big and strong and hurt the victim in a mental way.
- To make you feel you are just a wimp, nothing, a nobody. Your feelings are twisted and you feel like a nobody.

We returned to the improvisation to see how the scenario might conclude. As pupils worked in groups I laid pencils and paper in the spaces around the hall. Then pupils were asked to sit in a space next to a pencil and paper and write as the girl who was the victim. She had returned home and was about to write in her diary the entry for that day. What was in her thoughts? How was she feeling? It was the end of the session with only a few minutes to spare. In every case there was complete silence as pupils wrote in what turned out to be very thoughtful and emotional ways about how 'they' felt.

Session Three

The diary entries at the end of the last session were written anonymously. At the beginning of Session Three I read some of the entries back to the class. As in the previous week the process of reporting back to pupils helped to focus their thinking on the theme of these sessions and also reinforced a sense of ownership of their work and the development of their thinking. Whilst the first two sessions had dealt with individual bullying, in Session Three I wanted to concentrate on how differences in power between groups meant that bullying had a social dimension too.

We were working in the school hall, which I asked pupils to imagine was the playground. Together we constructed the imaginary scene so that everyone had an image of the hall as the school playground. It was time for the pupils to go out to play. I simply asked them to go into the playground and do what they normally did there. I watched them playing. They enacted football games, some were skipping, others chatted. I asked two or three girls to walk across the space where the boys were playing football. The reaction of the boys to the girls who had 'invaded their space' was hostile. Then I froze the action and asked pupils to look around. What did they notice? It was usually the girls who commented on how little space they had; how the boys dominated the playground and how the girls were often forced to its fringes. These observations led to a debate about gender relations in school. The boys often defended themselves by saying they didn't mind girls playing football too. Those girls who had played commented that the boys only partially included them in the game because they did not pass the ball to them. We talked about why boys often assumed they had a right to dominate space and went on to consider ways in which the playground could be shared more equitably.

I explicitly made the point that one group's domination over another could be seen as social bullying and then asked pupils to sit in a space. After doing a concentration exercise I read the book *The Children We Remember*. It is an incredibly evocative book, written in simple language, and tells the story of the fate of Jewish children during the Holocaust. At the end of the story, I didn't need to ask pupils to reflect on what they had heard, they were already doing that, such was the power of the narrative. All I asked was for them to write a response to the story. This is what some of them wrote:

- It was a sad story and a terrible thing to do. What a short life for those poor children. They wiped out the whole town.
- The Nazis almost wiped out a whole generation of Jews. I think it's terrible what the Nazis did. Those children will never forget what they did. The worst thing is it was all true.
- I think it was cruel and unnecessary to those people, just because they were a different religion. The bullies acted as though they were superior to the Jews. It was disgusting and should never have happened.
- I think it was a sad story and it made you think how lucky we really are . . .
- . . . I would have helped the Jewish people, even if it meant death for me, because they should not have been treated like that just because they were a different religion to others.
- I think the Nazis are cruel, unloving people. I do not know why they did it, but whatever it was it was racist.
- . . . I feel sorry for them because their lives were wasted.
- But we were as bad to the Nazis' children. We should have fought the war on our own and left the children. The children suffered for our mistakes and our war. They should have been left to play and talk to their friends or be alone, but we made them suffer.
- I think it will always be a nightmare for those people and those children that are now adults.
- I feel the story brings out the cruelty of life and shows how unfair certain people are. It makes me so angry when I hear stories like this . . .
- I think that shows that some people can be very nasty to people with a different religion and I don't think that's fair. Everybody should be treated the same way as other people . . .

The story and all the work that led up to it enabled pupils to reflect deeply. Some of them responded specifically to the story, whilst others were able to make a generalised statement about justice and human rights. One response, however, served as an abrupt reminder that no matter how much work is done in the classroom, there will be a tiny minority who are impervious to empathy and social justice. One pupil in one school wrote:

- The Germans will be Germans. It is all in the past now so we can forget about it. I don't really care. Hitler rules OK.

This response is chillingly similar to the revisionist position of neo-Nazis, and we need to remind ourselves that Nazism was not restricted to Germany; like modern terrorism it had its cells and sympathisers in most European countries, including Britain. Nor is it a thing of the past, as the anti-fascist journal *Searchlight* constantly reminds us. It is inevitable therefore that some teachers will encounter pupils who come from families where neo-Nazi doctrine is accepted. It is highly unlikely that we will change such entrenched attitudes. What we must do is make the majority aware of the dangers of allowing bullies to become powerful and that such people, when organised, can use democracy to their advantage. I demonstrated how easy it is for democracy to be turned to dictatorship by asking one third of the class to stand. This was all it took, 33 per cent of the vote, to give the Nazis power in the German parliament.

Session Four

During the first three sessions pupils had explored some of the affective and political implications of bullying, both for individuals and for whole groups of people. We had constructed an implicit rationale for doing something about bullying, and in the final session we discussed what could be done to prevent or stop bullying from occurring, firstly as individuals and then as a whole class. Pupils wrote that an individual response to bullying might include the following actions:

- I can't do anything on my own, but I can tell other people so they can help stop them in a group.
- Don't fight back tell someone in authority.
- Use words to put them in their place.
- Make sure I don't say or be nasty to people. Stop friends bullying people.
- I can try to convince people that bullying is cruel, but it has to be their choice because if they really want to stop, they can do it on their own.
- I could stick up for the person who is being bullied and try to make the bully think about what they are doing to the other person.
- I could get a lot of people who didn't want that person to carry on calling names and say that you won't have any friends if you carry on.
- Tell younger people and some older ones what they mean when they call people names and to think about what they are saying.
- Be kind to everyone and make sure I don't bully anyone. I could put a good example to everybody younger than me.
- First I would try and sort it out myself by talking to them about it and if that didn't work I would tell someone else, hoping they could do something about it.

Many of these examples show a sense of personal responsibility: an empowerment to do something about bullying. The importance of talk, the effect of group involvement, and the recognition that telling someone about the problem helps, may well have been influenced by the use of open discussion and collaborative learning strategies in the project itself. This would suggest that the strategies and processes used for teaching and learning are as important to the development of thought as the knowledge and concepts that form the content of lessons. However, not all pupils responded quite so positively. Some thought that nothing could be done to stop bullying; that if someone was intent on bullying they would do it. In order to encourage further reflection on positive action, I included with the written feedback to pupils two questions:

- Which actions do you think have the most chance of being successful?
- Which actions do you think would have no effect?

I had hoped the realisation that doing nothing about bullying has no effect would lead these pupils back to a consideration of positive measures to tackle the problem. Many of the suggestions of action the whole class could take to stop bullying implied that pupils felt more empowered as part of a group because fewer of them said nothing could be done. Some pupils recognised that as the oldest children in the school they were in a position to model positive behaviour. The following responses were typical of their thinking:

- We can set an example by talking things out with each other and not fighting it out.
- Our classes could stop bullying and calling names and maybe younger people will catch on.
- Encourage people to stop bullying and calling each other names by setting an example to the younger years or everybody.

Other pupils suggested a more systematic approach, including:

- Doing an assembly in front of the whole school and telling them how it would feel.
- Set up a bullying patrol. Every playtime people in the class look out for bullies and when they get in tell their teacher. Compile a list of people and if they are persistent, keep them in at playtime.
- We could look out for the bullies and when we get back to class write it down on a chart like this,

Victim	Suspect bully	Time	Name of observer

Then at the end of a certain period look at the chart and see what you could find out. If someone bullied more than a certain amount of time they go to the Headteacher.

Clearly some pupils had recognised that harassment becomes bullying when it is persistent behaviour and that bullying can be detected by means of careful monitoring and recording of incidents.

End note

Each class presented their work in various ways. Some produced booklets or wall displays, others did indeed share their work with the whole school during assembly time. Early in the project a short anti-bullying rap was devised, which synthesised much of the thinking that emerged during discussions with pupils. It is reproduced below:

Message to the Child Who Stands Alone

Don't let the bullies get their way,
Don't keep silent, have your say.
They want you to be weak and small,
So tell someone or you'll feel awful.
Your name is your name, wear it with pride,
Don't be abused, you'll hurt inside.
Stand up, stand up, don't lose face,
If they abuse your class, sex or race.
The bully looks big and shouts a lot
But when you get to it they're not that hot.
Don't stand alone, don't be afraid,
Don't let your life a hell be made
By the bully, the one who calls you a bad name,
Bullying and name calling are serious, no game,
So don't silently suffer, find your voice,
What you want to be called is your choice.

The strategies outlined in this project seemed to be effective with older Key Stage Two and early Key Stage Three pupils. However, the longer-term effects of such work would need to be judged by research capable of measuring changes in behaviour and attitudes to bullying and name-calling. Teachers of younger pupils may feel these strategies might not work and that alternative approaches are needed. To this end, teachers of pupils in Foundation, Key Stage One and early Key Stage Two might find the work of Babette Brown useful. Babette Brown's introduction to Britain of 'persona dolls' has influenced a number of practitioners who work with younger pupils in multi-ethnic areas, although they can be used with any group of pupils. In the next chapter, I draw on the experience of a former colleague of mine who has used persona dolls extensively in her work.

7 Persona dolls

Persona dolls have proved to be a powerful means of challenging 'the values, stereotypes and prejudices that underpin racism and other social inequalities' (Brown 2000). The dolls are given individual biographies which are shared with pupils. Through the telling of a life story, the doll becomes a 'living being' to whom children can relate. Once pupils have befriended the doll, it can be used as a vehicle to raise, discuss and resolve difficult issues and concerns that children experience in their lives. The fact that it is the doll that has the difficulty distances children from any emotional problems they might be experiencing in their personal lives and enables them to view a problem with empathy and a degree of objectivity. Solutions that children provide to problems are valued and treated with respect, which helps raise the child's confidence and self-esteem.

Brown (2001) acknowledges three theoretical sources for the use of persona dolls. Firstly, she cites the libertarian pedagogy of Paulo Freire, which emphasised teaching methods that involved 'problem-solving practice'. Such teaching methods lead to individual and collective empowerment. The second source is constructivist learning theories such as those of Bruner and Vygotsky, which advocate the creation of knowledge through dialogue with others. Thirdly, she draws on the work of Louise Derman-Sparks, which emphasises the creation of egalitarian approaches to learning. These are approaches that encourage all children to know about and appreciate their own identity and culture without feeling superior to others.

Stages in developing persona dolls

Dolls can be bought, but good practice in the use of persona dolls indicates that it is far better for parents to be involved in the making of the dolls and the creation of their biographies.

Stage one – making dolls

The doll's appearance needs to be realistic and avoid caricature. It is advised that the skin tones, eye shape and hair texture of dolls are similar to the range of physical characteristics of pupils in the class.

Stage two – devising a persona

The biography of each doll should be authentic and reflect appropriate cultural, linguistic and religious factors associated with its ethnicity. As with appearance, the dolls should be representative of the ethnic mix of the class. Minority ethnic parents and members of the local community are an invaluable source of advice when creating the doll's persona.

Stage Three – naming the doll

The name given to the doll also needs to be authentic. Once again, parents can be asked to offer suggestions that are appropriate to the gender and ethnicity of the doll.

Stage Four – befriending the doll

It is advised that dolls are introduced one at a time so that children can begin to develop a relationship with each doll. Part of the doll's biography is told to the children and then the doll is given its own chair. The doll sits in the classroom and can be cuddled and or spoken to by a child at any time.

Stage Five – developing empathy

Once children have befriended the doll, more of its life history is told. More importantly, the doll is used to introduce and discuss problems. These problems can be reactive or proactive, that is, a manifest problem can be raised for discussion, or a problem that has not arisen in class or in the school could be used to stimulate thought. The essential point is that by using the doll, teachers are able to facilitate discussion, actively listen to children's responses and support pupils when required. For their part children identify the doll's feelings, share ideas and offer the doll advice. Any misinformation and prejudices that emerge in children's discussion are noted by the teacher who provides correct information and alternative ways of thinking at a later stage.

Persona dolls in action

Two former colleagues of mine, Rita Gist and Linda Bartlett of the Milton Keynes Ethnic Minority Support Service (EMASS), have found persona dolls to be an effective means of encouraging empathy in young children. After being introduced to the concept and methodology of persona dolls at one of Babette Brown's training sessions, Linda set up an African and African Caribbean parents support group. The group was enthused by the idea of the dolls and began to make several. Rita explained the process as follows:

> The parents sewed the dolls at home, they found suitable wool for their hair and experimented with eyes, noses and mouths. The result was dolls with differing features, which we were worried about at first. But which the children accept because '. . . everybody is different' and 'you mustn't judge people by the way they look'. The dolls were kitted out in suitable clothes and shoes from second-hand shops. Then they were brought along to a subsequent Parents' group meeting where they were given names. The group then began to create personal histories.
>
> In group brainstorming sessions, parents volunteered ideas while one person scribed. We were able to draw on the parents' cultural backgrounds and acknowledge family life in the Caribbean or African country represented by the doll. This helped to create authentic

family histories for the dolls with anecdotal stories of holidays in Jamaica etc. The notes were taken away and word-processed. The EMASS team now has five dolls with accompanying personal histories for use in local schools.

Through her practical work with the dolls, Rita has identified the following learning objectives:

- To introduce children to social diversity.
- To present positive images of Black children and their families.
- To help children gain an awareness and understanding of the richness and variety of different lifestyles.
- To make the different backgrounds of children visible to others in the group.
- To enable children to discover what they have in common with those from different ethnic backgrounds.
- To provide opportunities for children to see their own individuality and life experiences valued, thereby building self-esteem.
- To enable children to identify with and relate to the personality created through the doll.
- To help develop non-discriminatory attitudes and understandings within children.
- To tackle issues (such as name-calling or rejection of a pupil) which have arisen in school.
- To encourage children to consider the feelings of others, empathise and give advice, without personalising the situation.
- To help children learn self-help strategies for dealing with perceived unfairness.

Babette Brown offers training in the use of persona dolls. Further details are available at Persona Doll Training, 51 Granville Road, London N12 0JH.

8 The Forgotten Heroine: The Journey of Mary Seacole

Teacher's notes

Introduction

The following short playscript is based on the life of the Jamaican nurse, Mary Seacole, who, like her contemporary, Florence Nightingale, went to the Crimea to nurse British soldiers when war broke out in 1854. Whereas Florence Nightingale is respected as a heroine and is even referred to in schemes of work devised by the Qualification and Curriculum Authority (QCA), Mary Seacole has been virtually forgotten.

There may be two possible reasons why one woman is remembered whilst the other has been forgotten. Both are to do with power and inequality. Mary was relatively poor, the daughter of a Jamaican nurse and a Scottish soldier; Florence on the other hand was well connected, being the sister-in-law of Sir Henry Verney, whose country home was Claydon House in Buckinghamshire, where Florence had her own special room. Mary's struggle to achieve her vocation was far greater than Florence Nightingale's; she not only had to raise money for her journey, firstly from Jamaica to London and then from England to the Crimea, but also she had to overcome the daunting hurdles of prejudice and racism. It is possible to conclude then that differences of 'race' and class between the two women are the reasons why Florence Nightingale achieved fame whilst Mary Seacole did not.

In recent years, scholars have begun to explore the forgotten heroes of the past; those who because of their gender, 'race' or class were deemed unworthy of having their stories told. Even today, many of these people, like Mary Seacole, remain on the margins of mass awareness. The playscript deals with the theme of the forgotten and raises the question as to why it is that some people become legends whilst others do not. The purpose of drama is to raise questions. After a reading of the script the play's theme could be followed up through extension work. This might include a comparison of the lives of Florence Nightingale and Mary Seacole with the central question under investigation being the reason why Mary was forgotten. Florence Nightingale's life and works are well documented so I have suggested below some sources that pupils and teachers could use to investigate the life and works of Mary Seacole.

Further reading on the life of Mary Seacole

Seacole, M. *The Wonderful Adventures of Mrs. Seacole*. Various editions.
File, N., and Power, C. (1995) *Black Settlers in Britain, 1555–1958*. Oxford: Heinemann.
Fryer, P. (1984) *Staying Power: The History of Black People in Britain*. London: Pluto Press.

Useful websites

There are almost 100 websites featuring Mary Seacole. Many of them contain the same information, albeit for different age groups and reading levels. The following brief selection provides a starting point for further research on Mary's life. The Westminster site includes a storyboard display of Mary's life produced by primary age pupils.

www.btinternet.com/~ardena/mary-seacole

www.chronicleworld.org/tomsite/capsule

www.ds.dial.pipex.com/town/terrace/lf41/na/june00/fo

www.dmu.ac.uk/Schools/HCS/MSRC/ who_was_mary_seacole

www.internurse.com/history/seacole

www.wgfl.westminster.gov.uk/resources/bhm/mary-seacole.htm

THE FORGOTTEN HEROINE: THE JOURNEY OF MARY SEACOLE

Scene One: A sitting room

As the lights go up a man can be seen, seated in an old armchair, to one side of the stage. He is holding a book, which he has been reading. As he looks up thoughtfully, he lays the book on his lap and speaks as though to someone who cannot be seen.

Man: It seems to me that history is full of people, men and women, who have made sacrifices in their own lives to help others. Sometimes these people are held up as examples to us all. Some of them have books written about them. Some of them become the heroes of our past. But others, what becomes of them? Their acts of heroism become lost and forgotten. Why should that be? Why should one person's sacrifice be revered by future generations? Why should one person's life become legendary whilst another's is lost beyond all memory? What if the forgotten heroes of the past could revisit us and tell their stories? What might we learn from them? (*He yawns and rests his head against the high back of the chair.*) If only it were possible to conjure a forgotten hero or heroine in dream. That way the forgotten could have their stories told by the living; that way they could be part of us again. (*He closes his eyes.*) And so to dream. (*He falls asleep.*)

The lights fade to represent the man sinking into a deep sleep. Slowly, a light blue spotlight illumines a figure at the back of the room. The light remains subdued and the figure, a woman, is mostly in shadow. She is wearing a long black dress. Her hair is short and thick. She stands upright and steps forward proudly. The spotlight follows her. She turns to face the man. As she does, a second spotlight illumines him. As the light intensifies he stirs in his sleep and speaks.

Man: Yes, to dream . . . forgotten heroes . . . heroic acts . . . forgotten stories.

Mary: Sleep. Sleep and rest. Gently, now. Listen. I have a story.

Man: You do?

Mary: A story of a long-forgotten woman. A woman who enters your dreams, not because she craves to be remembered for what she did. Not because she wants to become a legend, but because too many of us have been forgotten.

Man: Who are you?

Mary: Mary. I was Mary. I last trod this earth in 1881, during the reign of Queen Victoria. Today, I sleep in Kensal Rise Cemetery, in North London.

Man: Is that where you are from?

Mary: No. I did not always live in London. In fact, I came to England as a young woman. My father was Scottish, but I wasn't born in Scotland either. He was a soldier. He met my mother when he went to Jamaica with the British Army. He sailed all the way across the Atlantic Ocean to the Caribbean. That's where I was born, in Kingston, Jamaica. Ah, this is me with my mother, now.

Spotlights illumine a section of the stage. A woman enters with a girl at her side. The woman carries a small basket. She takes a phial from the basket and hands it to the girl.

Mother: Mary, take this medicine and give it to the sick soldier over there, it will help make him well again. (*The girl takes the phial and crosses to where the man is sleeping.*)

Mary: Here, drink this. Mother says it will help you get well. (*Mary lifts the phial to the man's lips and he slowly drinks the liquid.*)

Man: Thank you child. Your mother is an angel and you will be one too.

Mary returns to her mother's side.

Mary: What's the matter with him? Is he so ill?

Mother: Cholera, my dear. A dreadful disease.

Mary: How will the liquid help, will it cure him?

Mother: If we have caught it in time he will survive.

Mary: How do you know how to cure people?

Mother: Look around you. Look at the trees and plants, the herbs and spices. They all hold the key to life. It's a case of knowing which ailment can be cured by which plant. (*She takes several spices from her basket.*) The root of the ginger plant wards off colds and influenza, turmeric is an antiseptic, which heals cuts and burns . . .

Mary: Can I learn too, can I learn how to cure people?

Mother: You will learn. I will teach you everything I know.

The lights fade on the mother and the man, leaving Mary in a pool of light, centre stage.

Mary: The older I grew the more my mother taught me. I learned how to use the plants to cure all kinds of illnesses. Most of my patients were British soldiers who were stationed in Jamaica. But then war broke out in the Crimea and the soldiers left Jamaica for the battlefields in Russia. The year was 1854.

As the light fades on Mary, a second light illumines a newspaper vendor. He is holding up that day's newspaper.

News vendor: Read all about it! Read all about it! Thousands die in the Crimea. No bandages for the wounded. Sidney Herbert sets up fund. Florence Nightingale calls for help.

The light fades on the news vendor and Mary, older now, is once again in the spotlight.

Mary: News came to me that the soldiers were suffering terrible conditions in the Crimea. There were no hospitals to house the wounded. The sick and dying were left in the cold with no-one to tend to them. There were few doctors and even fewer nurses. I had to do something. I was a nurse and desperate people needed me. Without hesitation I collected my money, boarded a ship and sailed for England.

The light fades, leaving the stage in complete darkness.

Scene Two: The enlistment centre

A notice reads, 'Recruiting Today: Nurses for the Crimean War'. Below it are three chairs. Mary enters. She is carrying a large bag. She walks past the chairs, stops, and walks back again. A man enters. He looks official and is carrying some official-looking documents.

Official man: Can I help you madam?

Mary: I am a nurse. I heard that you desperately needed nurses for the Crimea. So I have come all the way from Jamaica to offer my services.

Official man (*unimpressed*): What is your name?

Mary: Mary. Mary Seacole.

Official man: Take a seat Miss Seacole. You will be called for interview shortly.

Mary sits as the man exits. Two women enter and sit on the empty chairs next to Mary. The man returns. He approaches the two women who have just entered.

Official man (*smiling*): Good afternoon ladies. I assume you are offering your services for the Crimea.

First woman: Yes, indeed. I think it's terrible what our poor lads are suffering over there.

Second woman: Me too. You wouldn't let a dog die in those conditions.

Official man: Indeed, indeed. May I take your names.

First woman: Miss Read.

Second woman: Miss O'Sullivan.

Official man: Well, Miss Read, I think we are just about ready for the first interview. So, if you care to follow me, we'll get started. We will be with you shortly, Miss O'Sullivan.

Miss O'Sullivan nods politely. The man and Miss Read exit. There is now an empty seat between Mary and the other woman. Time passes. The two women sit in silence. After a while the man enters with Miss Read.

Official man: Thank you, Miss Read. I am sure our soldiers will welcome you, and may I wish you as pleasant a journey as our troop carriers are able to afford.

Miss Read exits, after smiling briefly at Miss O'Sullivan.

Official man: Miss O'Sullivan, you are next.

Miss O'Sullivan rises. She looks awkwardly at Mary, who sits impassively staring into space. The man and Miss O'Sullivan exit, leaving Mary alone. As time passes, Mary becomes impatient. She stands, paces up and down, looks in the direction of the interview room, paces again and then sits. Eventually the man and Miss O'Sullivan re-enter.

Official man: Once again, congratulations Miss O'Sullivan. Your ship will depart for the Crimea on Tuesday morning. You need to be at the quayside by 9 o'clock.

Miss O'Sullivan: I'll be there, bright and early.

As she leaves, Miss O'Sullivan gives Mary an embarrassed smile. Mary nods politely in response. The man ignores Mary and exits. Mary begins to look agitated as time passes. After a while the man re-enters. When he sees Mary he stops, looks at her and doubles back. Mary looks in the direction he went. There are voices off-stage.

Voice: Is that it, just two nurses?

Official man: Well, sir, there is a third. She has been waiting rather a long time but . . .

Voice: Show her in, show her in. Don't keep the woman waiting. We need all the hands we can get.

Official man: But sir, she is not suitable.

Voice: I'll be the judge of that, my good man. Show her in.

Official man: Sir, she is from the colonies.

Voice: So? Our colonial women are a hardy breed.

Official man: No, sir. She is not one of our women, she is Black.

Pause.

Voice: I see. Better send her away then.

On hearing this Mary stands proudly. She holds herself in a very dignified manner. To the audience she says:

Mary: I heard every word with my own ears. Foul voices in the darkness, uttering foul words to deny my very being. (*She turns to where the voices came from.*) What strange people you are. You are crying out for nurses but you will not speak to me because I am Black. Your soldiers are dying and you will not let me heal them because I am Black. Are your eyes so shrouded in White mists of prejudice that you cannot see the person in me? I will not be beaten by your bigotry. I will tend to the sick and dying. That is my destiny.

The lights fade until the stage is in total darkness.

Scene Three: A battlefield

Cannon-fire can be heard in the distance. As the lights come up wounded soldiers sit and lie on the ground. Mary Seacole moves amongst them, tending to their wounds.

Soldier: Mother, help me mother, help me. (*Mary goes to him.*)

Mary: Let me put this ointment on your wounds. It will take away the heat and help them heal. (*She bandages the wounds.*)

Soldier: Thank you. You are an angel.

Second soldier. Thank heaven for you Mary. Without you we would be lost souls.

Third soldier: God bless you Mary.

Fourth soldier: We'll never forget you Mary.

Second soldier: That we won't, you'll stay in our hearts forever.

A fifth soldier emerges from the shadows and walks down through the battlefield towards the audience. He resembles the man sat in the chair at the beginning of the play. As he speaks the lights slowly fade on the battleground scene.

Fifth soldier: Soon, every soldier knew of the heroism of Mary Seacole. When the war ended she returned with the troops to London, penniless. The Government poured praise on her contemporary, Florence Nightingale. Nothing was said of Mary. But the soldiers held her in their hearts, as they had said they would. They protested about the injustice of it all. One wrote to *The Times*:

> While the good deeds of Florence Nightingale are being praised, the actions of Mrs. Seacole are being forgotten. Will no one remember all the good work she did?

If high-standing ministers held her in such low regard, the same could not be said of ordinary people. A benefit concert was held in Mary's honour at the Royal Surrey Gardens. On each night for four nights 10,000 people packed the audience. A lot of money was raised, but Mary received only a small fraction of it. The soldiers had not forgotten Mary but when they grew old and died the public memory of Mary Seacole died with them. And so it is that the writers of history have given us stories of the good deeds of Florence Nightingale but the good deeds of Mary Seacole have long been forgotten. And why? Why should it be that one woman's good deeds are legendary whilst another's are lost in time? Perhaps in death as well as in life the woman that was Good Mother Seacole was hidden in the White mist of prejudice.

After a pause, the light slowly fades on the soldier. The stage is left in complete darkness.

Glossary

The language of multicultural education can be something of a minefield. A single word can have different meanings for different people. Sometimes words are used synonymously when their semantics are quite distinct. This brief glossary is provided to help clarify the meanings of some of those words.

Ethnic/ethnicity   The terms ethnic and 'race' are often used synonymously, but are semantically distinct. An ethnic group is so defined because its members share a common history that has evolved cultural practices, customs, beliefs and traditions. The group also usually has a common language. These factors make the group distinct from other groups, and it is usual for the group to be self-perpetuating. However, Fenton (1999) notes that ethnic identities are subject to change and redefinition. In multicultural societies, such as Britain, ethnicity can be viewed as a social process rather than as rigidly defined groupings. As cultural boundaries change, partly as a result of cross-cultural infusion, individuals and groups evolve new identities. Whilst members of ethnic groups may have broad social, linguistic, religious and cultural features in common, they may also have distinct differences. Within ethnic groups, therefore, there can be great diversity. A failure to recognise this diversity is likely to result in individuals being treated stereotypically.

Ethnocentric   The term ethnocentric refers to perceiving the world exclusively through the 'lens' of one's own culture, without regard for other cultures, or acknowledging the possibility of other cultural perspectives. In this sense, one's own culture is implicitly or explicitly regarded as being of greater value or superior to others. A curriculum can be ethnocentric if it exclusively reflects knowledge and values from one culture, or fails to accurately represent a source of knowledge when it originates in, or is shared with, another culture.

'Race'   The term 'race' is a problematic one because its meaning has changed significantly over the last 400 years, but some modern usages of the word have retained pejorative historical connotations. For this reason, many writers place the word in inverted commas to signify its slippery semantics. Whilst it is now agreed the term refers to socially constructed categories of identification, it was once used to define people on the basis of assumed biological and cultural difference (Jary and Jary 1991). The hierarchical division of humanity into races with unequal attributes has since been discredited as a pseudo-science, but as an ideological construct this meaning of the term can still have a potent force in some quarters. In pseudoscientific theory it was believed a person's 'race' determined their personality, intellectual capacity and moral outlook, as well as the culture and social organisation of the group (Fenton 1999).

Racism Premised upon the notion that distinct and separate races exist and that these can be ordered hierarchically, racism involves the practical application of ideas, attitudes and assumptions that serve for one racial group to discredit or socially, politically or economically to disadvantage another. In its most virulent form, racism asserts that 'race' is based on biological differences between people and that certain 'races' are innately superior to others. Historically, this ideology resulted in the oppression and genocide of people deemed to be of an inferior 'race' by people who viewed themselves as a superordinate 'race'. The term racism then refers to the subjugation in various ways of one ethnic group by another.

Institutional racism Social institutions are governed by rule-bound behaviour. Institutional racism exists when the practices, procedures, social processes or organisational culture of an institution result in the unequal treatment of an individual or group because of their racial identity. Such unequal treatment may lead to an individual or group being disadvantaged or even excluded. Disadvantage or exclusion need not be intentional, and this gives rise to the possibility of institutional practices that are unwittingly racist.

The Macpherson Report of the inquiry into the racist murder of Stephen Lawrence offers an official definition. It states that institutional racism is

> the collective failure of an organisation to provide an appropriate and professional service to people because of their colour, culture or ethnic origin. It can be seen or detected in processes, attitudes and behaviour which amount to discrimination through unwitting prejudice, ignorance, thoughtlessness and racist stereotyping which disadvantage minority ethnic people. (Macpherson 1999)

Resources and advice

The paucity of available, mainstream, resources that are truly inclusive of our multicultural society means that teachers can often waste valuable hours of their time searching for appropriate sources to supplement the curriculum. For some, the task will be more daunting than others, especially for those who do not live in the metropolitan areas, and where multicultural bookshops and suppliers are unlikely to be found. This annotated directory of organisations, publishers and suppliers is intended to make the search a little easier. Only those bodies that have made a contribution to social justice, racial equality and multiculturalism have been included, although this is by no means an exhaustive list.

Listed in the 'Directory of Organisations' are several charities, such as ActionAid, Oxfam and Christian Aid. In addition to their campaigning work, these organisations produce cross-curricular materials on a range of relevant issues. Other organisations, such as Instead, have been included for the advice they can offer teachers and school policymakers.

Under the heading 'More Sources for Resources' are listed commercial bodies. Many of these have devoted themselves exclusively to the publication and supply of multicultural and anti-racist resources for schools. Several publishing houses, including Mantra, Tamarind and Trentham, began life from humble beginnings in the 1980s, but have since developed to become leaders in their field. Mantra specialises in dual-language books, whereas Tamarind produces storybooks and biographies, many of which are written by Verna Wilkins, the director of the company. Verna takes an interesting stance on her biographical subjects. Instead of writing about Black achievers from the past she prefers Black achievers who 'have a pulse'. Trentham Books, which includes as one of its directors Gillian Klein, a long-standing contributor to anti-racist initiatives, publishes books for teachers. Many of the listed companies are run by ex-teachers.

Where it has been feasible, a summary of each organisation's aims and purpose has been included to enable the reader to judge which bodies suit their particular needs. Commercial companies have been categorised according to the main items produced, i.e. if a company's main product is books, but it also sells artefacts, it is listed under the heading 'Books' but its other products are also mentioned.

DIRECTORY OF ORGANISATIONS

Action Aid Schools and Youth, Chataway House, Leach Road, Chard, Somerset TA20 1FR
Tel: 01460 238000
Email: deved@actionaid.org.uk
Web: www.actionaid.org

The charity Action Aid works with poor and marginalised people to overcome poverty and challenge its attendant causes, injustice and inequity. For the past ten years it has produced an increasing range of educational resources, which cover literacy, geography, modern foreign languages and global citizenship. Through its visiting teacher network, schools can call on guest speakers who are able to devise presentations on distant localities and development issues. To supplement one of its most widely used resources, *Chembakoli: India Village Life*, Action Aid has produced a special website, chembakoli.com. This will enable teachers and pupils to access new materials on the village. In addition, Action Aid produce multimedia resources and Big Books for literacy hour.

Advisory Council for the Education of Romany and Other Travellers, Moot House, The Stow, Harlow CM20 3AG
Tel: 01279 418666

AIMER

AIMER, or Access to Information on Multicultural Education, is a database containing materials donated by publishers and teachers. It provides a comprehensive collection of what is available in the field. However, the database is not a selection of recommended materials, and quality may vary, therefore. The directory of resources is based at Reading University Reading and Language Information Centre, Reading University, Bulmershe Court, Earley, Reading RG6 1HY.

Anne Frank Educational Trust, PO Box 11880, London N6 4LN
Tel: 020 8340 9077
Email: afet@afet.org.uk
Web: www.annefrank.org.uk

Using the diary of Anne Frank, the Trust aims to promote positive attitudes in young people towards difference, particularly in age, gender, ethnicity, religion and disability. It does this by means of its touring exhibitions, educational projects and teaching packs.

Anti-Racist Teacher Education Network (ARTEN), c/o Flat 5, 19 Hillbury Road, London SW17 8JT

ARTEN is a network committed to challenging racism and promoting race equality in initial teacher education and continuing professional development.

Anti-Slavery International, Thomas Clarkson House, The Stableyard, Broomgrove Road, London SW9 9TL
Tel: 020 7501 8920
Email: info@antislavery.org
Web: www.antislavery.org

Chocolate is consumed in vast quantities by the nation's children without them or us giving much thought to its production. Anti-Slavery International awakens us to the fact that in some countries cocoa is produced by means of slave labour. Through its campaigning work, the organisation raises awareness and invites people to challenge manufacturers to adopt ethical policies. This provides children with the opportunity to write persuasively to a real audience, i.e. chocolate and sweet manufacturers.

Black Childcare Network, 17 Brownhill Road, London SE6 2EG

Centre For Jewish Education, The Montagu Centre, 21 Maple Street, London W1T 4BE
Tel: 020 7580 0214
The Centre runs courses and produces resources on aspects of Judaism and the Holocaust.

Centre for Language in Primary Education, Webber Street, London SE1 8QW
Tel: 020 7401 3382
Email: info@clpe.co.uk

Since it was established nearly thirty years ago, the Centre has developed an international reputation for its work in the fields of language, literacy and assessment of language. In addition to its publications, the Centre's staff organise courses and conferences and provide advice on a range of language-related matters, including bilingualism. The Centre houses a library of over 20,000 volumes, which includes more than 16,000 children's books. CLPE publications draw on classroom-based research and include the journal *Language Matters*.

Christian Aid, PO Box 100, London SE1 7RT
Web: www.christian-aid.org.uk

Christian Aid is a relief and development agency, representing 40 British and Irish Churches. It works in some of the poorest regions of the world and aims to make communities self-sufficient. In addition to its fieldwork, Christian Aid has an educational arm too. Its website for children, www.globalgang.org.uk, includes a teachers' section with materials and printable lesson plans. It publishes a resources catalogue with materials suitable for all Key Stages. As well as book-based materials, there are inexpensive interactive games, including *The Debt Game* and *The Trading Game*, both of which simulate real-life scenarios that help children understand the structural features of poverty around the world. Some of Christian Aid's educational materials can be obtained free of charge, such as its *RE Curriculum for Global Citizenship*.

Collaborative Learning Project, 17 Barford Street, Islington, London N1 0QB
Tel: 020 7226 8885

From its roots in Inner London in 1983, the Project is now an independent, non-profitmaking educational trust. The Project develops, disseminates and promotes activities designed to encourage effective collaborative group work across the curriculum and all Key Stages. Although its materials are not essentially of a multicultural nature, the learning approaches advocated encourage the fostering of an inclusive classroom and provide talk-rich environments for EAL pupils. By sending an A4 SAE teachers can receive *Paperclip*, the Project bulletin, which lists all available collaborative learning materials. These can be purchased relatively cheaply. The Project director, Stuart Scott, also runs teachers' workshops on collaborative learning.

Commission on British Muslims and Islamophobia, 356 Holloway Road, London N7 6PA
Tel: 020 7609 8870
Email: bmicom@freenet.co.uk
Web: www.runnymedetrust.org/meb (This is the homepage of the Multi-Ethnic Britain Commission. On arrival click ISLAMOPHOBIA.)

With support from the Runnymede Trust and the Commission for Racial Equality, the Commission on British Muslims and Islamophobia was established in 1995. The Commission promotes policies and activities that challenge anti-Muslim prejudice and discrimination. Its publications, some of which are available on its website, unpack the nature of Islamophobia and offer advice on how to foster open-minded attitudes towards Islam. Following the events of 11 September 2001, which have increased anti-Muslim feeling in Britain, teachers will find these publications useful when dealing with closed attitudes towards Islam amongst some pupils.

Commission on the Future of Multi-Ethnic Britain, 133 Aldersgate Street, London EC1A 3JA
Tel: 020 7600 9666
Web: www.runnymedetrust.org/meb

The Commission was established by the Runnymede Trust in 1998. Its main purpose was to evaluate issues of race equality and cultural diversity in modern Britain. The report of its findings, entitled *The Future of Multi-Ethnic Britain*, was published by Profile Books in autumn

2000. The Commission's website contains discussion extracts which could be useful for staff training, as well as government responses to the report.

Commission for Racial Equality (CRE), Elliot House, 10/12 Allington Street, London SW1E 5EH
Tel: 020 7828 7022
Web: www.cre.gov.uk

The CRE has regional offices in Birmingham, Leeds and Manchester, as well as offices in Scotland and Wales. In addition, most towns and cities have local Racial Equality Councils.

Established by the 1976 Race Relations Act, the Commission for Racial Equality, which is funded by the Home Office but is independent of government, has a national brief to promote equality of opportunity through the elimination of racial discrimination. Working with organisations and companies, it offers advice and guidance on ways to avoid discrimination in employment, housing, education, the legal system and other service sector industries. Where evidence of unfair treatment on racial grounds occurs, the CRE is able to conduct formal investigations and order the implementation of changes. The CRE has made several investigations of Local Education Authorities and, as a result of its findings, has caused a number of discriminatory practices to cease, including the 'bussing' of Asian pupils to schools outside their own residential areas. Reports of these formal investigations are obtainable from the CRE.

The CRE also publishes educational materials. One publication that is of particular interest to teachers is *Roots of the Future*, a large-format book that chronicles migration to Britain, as well as the achievements of minority ethnic groups and individuals throughout history who have made Britain their home. Allied to the book is a set of 7 posters and a pack of 12 postcards, which can be ordered separately. The introduction to the book is accessible on the web, at www.cre.gov.uk/ethdiv/ed-roots.html. By downloading it onto the school's network the introduction could be used as a resource in its own right.

Useful CRE publications for professional development include:

Code of Practice for the Elimination of Racial Discrimination in Education
Ethnic Monitoring in Education
Exclusion from School and Racial Equality: A Good Practice Guide
From Cradle to School: A Practical Guide to Racial Equality in Early Childhood Education and Care
Inspecting Schools for Race Equality: OFSTED's Strengths and Weaknesses
Learning for All: Standards for Racial Equality in Schools
Set to Fail? Ethnic Minority Pupils in Secondary Education

Following the passing of the Race Relations (Amendment) Act 2000, the CRE has produced guidance to schools on the implementation of statutory duties to promote race equality. The full catalogue of publications can be viewed on CRE's website, which also includes a printable order form. Orders are dealt with by Central Books at the following address: Central Books, 99 Wallis Road, London E9 5LN. Tel: 020 8986 5488 Email: cre@centralbooks.com

Commonwealth Institute, Kensington High Street, London W8 6NQ
Tel: 020 7603 4535
Email: crc@commonwealth.org.uk
Web: www.commonwealth.org.uk

The Commonwealth Institute is an independent agency representing the cultures of the 54 nations that make up the Commonwealth. Consisting of nearly a third of the world's population, Commonwealth countries include diverse religions, languages and environments. The Institute's resource centre houses a collection of over 20,000 multimedia resources, including a comprehensive range of literature by Commonwealth writers. Annual membership enables members to borrow up to ten items per month.

Early Years Trainers Anti-Racist Network (EYTARN), PO Box 28, Wallasey CH45 9NP
Tel: 0151 639 6136

Football Unites, Racism Divides (furd), The Stables, Mount Pleasant Community Centre, Sharrow Lane, Sheffield S11 8AE
Tel: 0114 255 3156
Email: furd@furd.org
Web: www.furd.org

In 1995 a group of Sheffield Wednesday fans who had been concerned about racist incidents in and around their stadium founded furd with the aim to make football accessible to everyone without fear of racial abuse. Today, the project has an established website, a resource centre and a team of staff who run projects in the local community. With the kind of interest that young people have in football, organisations like furd and the national body, Kick Racism Out of Football, have a great deal to offer schools. Of particular interest is the project's biography of Arthur Wharton, Britain's first Black footballer, who played for Wednesday.

Instead, 14 Hugh Street, Wembley, Middlesex HA9 8DD
Tel: 020 8900 1720
Email: robin@instead.co.uk
        angela@instead.co.uk

Instead (Inservice Training and Educational Development) is a consultancy run by Robin Richardson and Angela Wood. Dealing mainly with issues of race equality and religious education, Instead provides an evaluation, training and management service to public bodies and the voluntary sector. Several of its projects have initiated publications, including:

Islamophobia: A Challenge For Us All (Runnymede Trust 1997).
Enriching Literacy (Trentham Books 1999)
Inclusive Schools, Inclusive Society (Trentham Books 1999)
Equality in Education (Slough Borough Council 1999)
Equity and Excellence (Royal Borough of Windsor and Maidenhead 2001)

Institute of Race Relations, 2–6 Leeke Street, London WC1X 9HS
Tel: 020 7837 0041
Email: info@irr.org.uk
Web: www.irr.org.uk

The Institute of Race Relations is an educational charity. Its main aim is to inform the struggle for racial justice in Britain and throughout the world. By means of thorough research and analysis, the Institute reflects the experiences of those who suffer racial oppression. It has produced a number of educational resources, including the superb *Homebeats*, a CD-Rom; a set of four books; a poster set and a simply written broadsheet. The CD-Rom is a well-presented, user-friendly educational resource, which includes valuable material about key figures from Black history as well as documentary material suitable for PSHE and Citizenship Education. A catalogue containing details of these materials is available on request. Staff at the Institute are available to demonstrate the CD-Rom in schools and youth centres. Also of interest is *Schools Against Deportations*, which records the successful involvement of schools and pupils in preventing the removal of refugee schoolmates. This information can be viewed on the organisation's website.

IQRA Trust, 24 Culross Street, London W1Y 3HE
Tel: 020 7491 1572
Email: info@iqratrust.org
Web: www.iqratrust.org

Founded in 1988, IQRA is a Muslim educational charity. It includes amongst its aims the promotion of greater understanding and mutual respect among Muslims and non-Muslims. The organisation has devised an interactive multimedia exhibition for use by LEAs, depicting the Islamic faith and its history. It also provides INSET and publishes resources for all Key Stages.

Jewish Council for Racial Equality, 33 Seymour Place, London W1H 6AT
Tel: 020 8455 0896
Email: jcore@btinternet.com

Since it was founded in 1976 JCORE has worked with other organisations to fight racial injustice and build a just and harmonious multicultural society. It has produced anti-racist educational materials for both primary and secondary-aged pupils. For Key Stages One and Two there is *Let's Make a Difference*, and the secondary equivalent is *Jewish Perspectives on Racism*.

Kick It Out, Unit 3, 1–4 Christina Street, London EC2A 4PA
Tel: 020 7684 4884
Email: kick-racism@kick-it-out.demon.co.uk
Web: www.kickitout.org

Kick It Out was launched by the Commission for Racial Equality and the Football Association in 1993. As an independent organisation it promotes the 'Let's Kick Racism Out of Football' campaign, which seeks to eradicate racism from all levels of football.

Letterbox Library, 71–3 Allen Road, London N16 8RY
Tel: 020 7503 4801
Email: info.letterboxlibrary.com
Web: www.letterboxlibrary.com

Run as a workers' cooperative, Letterbox Library has existed for about 18 years. It specialises in non-sexist and multicultural books for children, which are advertised through its quarterly magazine. Although membership is not required, with a one-off joining fee of £5 members are able to get discounts of up to 12.5 per cent on special offers. An independent panel of reviewers, including librarians, parents, teachers and children, carefully selects books to feature in the magazine. They look for excellence in terms of storylines, content, characterisation, illustrations and texts that depict the diversity of our multicultural world and show people of different gender, 'race' and ethnicity in non-stereotypical ways. The selection in each magazine covers a wide age range from picture books for the very young to adult fiction. There is also a category for 'reluctant readers' and cross-curricular resources.

Mediation UK, Alexander House, Telephone Avenue, Bristol BS1 4BS
Web: www.mediationuk.org.uk

Founded in 1984, Mediation UK is a national charity which represents and supports mediation and conflict resolution within local communities. It also works in schools where it trains pupils to become peer mediators who are then able to assist other pupils to resolve quarrels and prevent bullying. The organisation's website includes examples of successful practice, as well as contacts for other similar organisations.

Minority Rights Group, 379 Brixton Road, London SW9 7DE
Tel: 020 7978 9498
Email: minority.rights@mrgmail.org
Web: www.minorityrights.org

Founded over 25 years ago, MRG is an international non-governmental organisation that promotes the rights of ethnic, linguistic and religious minorities throughout the world. The organisation has four main objectives, which are:

- To research and publish reports and other information about minorities around the world.
- To promote the rights of minorities at the UN, in Europe and with national governments.
- To educate teachers and pupils on minority issues in order to counter racism and prejudice.
- To build alliances with similar organisations to further the rights of minorities worldwide.

MRG produces educational materials which can be ordered via its website. Materials of particular interest to teachers include:

- the photo-pack *Travellers in Britain*;
- the poster of Pastor Niemoeller's poem 'First they came for the Jews';
- *Forging New Identities:* a booklet in which young refugees and minority students tell their stories;

- a series of booklets under the generic title, *Voices From*, which include autobiographical accounts of young refugees from various countries.

The *Voices From* series includes dual-language booklets, which provide authentic material for modern foreign languages. The materials are also useful for modelling autobiographical writing in English and as secondary source material for the study of a distant place in geography.

Mirage, Park Walk Primary School, Park Walk, London SW10 0AY
Tel: 020 7349 9969
Email: mir:arts@dircon.co.uk

Mirage is a non-profitmaking multicultural arts organisation. Its members perform live for schools and conduct storytelling workshops for teachers and librarians. It also produces dual-language cassette tapes of traditional stories in languages ranging from Albanian to Urdu.

NASSEA, c/o Ethnic Minority Achievement Service, TEDC, Lakes Road, Dukinfield SK16 4TR
Tel: 0161 331 3153

NASSEA is the Northern Association of Support Services for Equality and Achievement. Its work includes the publication of the influential *EAL Assessment: Guidance on the NASSEA EAL Assessment System*, which is being adopted by EMASS teams around the country. The NASSEA document builds on the assessment guidance for EAL pupils in the early stages of acquiring English, published in *A Language in Common* by QCA, but is more comprehensive because it includes assessment levels that are comparable to National Curriculum levels in English up to Levels 4 and 5.

National Association for Language Development in the Curriculum (NALDIC), South Hertfordshire LCSC, Holywell School Site, Tolpits Lane, Watford WD1 8NT
Tel: 01923 231855
Web: www.naldic.org.uk

Formed in 1993 by classroom teachers and EMTAG staff, NALDIC is a professional body for teachers interested in raising the achievement of pupils with English as an additional language. One of NALDIC's aims is to disseminate information about good practice in language-teaching through the curriculum. The organisation publishes a termly newsletter and holds an annual conference for members. At a regional level, members share ideas, materials and teaching strategies.

National Association of Teachers of Travellers, c/o WMESTEC, The Graiseley Centre, Pool Street, Wolverhampton WV2 4NE
Tel: 01902 714646

Oxfam, 274 Banbury Road, Oxford OX2 7DZ
Tel: 01865 313600
Email: Oxfam@oxfam.org.uk

The well-known charity Oxfam has a comprehensive range of resources that have been carefully selected by its education advisers. Its catalogue can be obtained in hard copy or via the web, either at the above address or through its dedicated site for teachers and pupils at www.oxfam.org.uk/coolplanet. Through its education wing, Oxfam aims to bring global issues into the classroom by means of active learning methods. Such methods include the use of games, simulation activities, video and CD-Rom. Its range of resources covers all Key Stages and most curriculum subjects. In addition to its headquarters in Oxford, Oxfam has regional centres around Britain. It also has links with numerous local Development Education Centres, which are listed in its catalogue.

Race on the Agenda, 356 Holloway Road, London N7 6PA
Tel: 020 7700 8135
Email: rota@rota.org.uk
Web: www.rota.org.uk
ROTA is a policy development, information and research service for the Black voluntary sector in London.

Working with other organisations and key policymakers, ROTA seeks to eliminate racial discrimination in the capital by promoting best practice in equal opportunities. Its work covers all the social and community sectors. Within education it works with LEAs and has run a project looking at the achievement and exclusion of Black children in London schools. Out of its work came the publication *Inclusive Schools, Inclusive Society*, by Robin Richardson and Angela Woods.

Refugee Council, 3 Bondway, London SW8 1SJ
Tel: 020 7820 3042
Email: info@refugeecouncil.org.uk

The Refugee Council gives practical help to asylum seekers and refugees, as well as promoting their rights in Britain and abroad. On the educational front the Council is able to provide training for teachers, published materials and advice. Teachers can seek further information from the National Education Adviser on 020 7820 3108. In addition to free materials, the Council's catalogue of teaching resources includes the following:

- A1 'Welcome' poster in different refugee languages;
- bilingual word books and stories;
- Literacy Hour work;
- books on helping pupils psychologically affected by war and displacement.

Runnymede Trust, Suite 106, The London Fruit and Wool Exchange, Brushfield St, London E1 6EP
Tel: 020 7377 9222
Email: Runnymede@trt.demon.co.uk
Web: www.runnymedetrust.org

Founded in 1968, the Runnymede Trust is an independent think tank with a mission to challenge racial discrimination, influence anti-racist legislation and promote a successful multi-ethnic Britain. The Trust is particularly concerned to develop strategies to raise the educational achievement of minority ethnic pupils. It has several publications on issues related to youth and education, including:

Examining School Exclusions and the Race Factor (1999)
Improving Practice: A Whole School Approach to Raising the Achievement of African Caribbean Youth (1998)
Black and Ethnic Minority Young People and Educational Disadvantage (1997)
Equality Assurance in Schools (2001, revised edn)

Salusbury World, Refugee Centre, Salusbury Primary School, Salusbury Road, London NW6 6RG
Tel: 020 7372 2244
Email: ninchohda@salusbury.brent.sch.uk

Regarded as a model for schools with high intakes of refugee pupils, the refugee centre was established to serve the needs of refugee children, their parents and communities.

Save the Children, 17 Grove Lane, London SE5 8RD
Tel: 020 7703 5400
Email: j.marsh@scfuk.org.uk
Web: www.savethechildren.org.uk

Save the Children is a registered charity. It has two catalogues of published resources: one for the under-twelves and the other for young people aged 12–18. Although not all resources are exclusively of a multicultural nature, they do adhere to an inclusive ethos and there is some good material designed to promote anti-discriminatory behaviour in children and young people. As might be expected, the emphasis in these resources is on children's perspectives, which makes them invaluable resources for the classroom. In addition to book-based resources, Save the Children also publishes poster sets, including 'Our Wide World' and 'Our Changing World'.

Shap Working Party on World Religions in Education, c/o The National Society Religious Education Centre, 36 Causton Street, London SW1P 4AU
Tel: 020 7932 1190

Established in 1969 at a conference at the Shap Wells Hotel, Cumbria, the Shap Working Party produces an annual calendar of religious festivals. This colourful resource is an invaluable reminder of the dates of holy days and festivals of some of the major religions in this country.

Support and Training Against Racism for Under Fives, Workers and Parents (STAR), 7 Barton Buildings, Bath BA1 2JR
Tel: 01225 334415

Working Group Against Racism in Children's Resources (WGARCR), 460 Wandsworth Road, London SW8 3LX
Tel: 020 7627 4594

The working group provides an advocacy service as well as advice and support to families and children experiencing racial harassment and exclusion from school. It also works to promote the use of positive images in resources.

MORE SOURCES FOR RESOURCES

Art

Alexandra Galleries, 340 Camberwell New Road, Camberwell Green, London SE5 0RW
Tel: 020 7274 0900
Email: alxgallery@aol.com

Supplier of African-American prints and posters.

Visual Art, 96 Turner Road, Edgware, Middlesex HA8 6BH
Tel: 020 8930 1783
Email: vaishali47@hotmail.com

Dealer in paintings, sculptures, graphics and prints.

Artefacts

Artefacts to Order and **A Suitcase of History**
Tel: 01945 587452
Email: educational.artefacts@bigfoot.com
Web: www.artefacts.demon.co.uk

Supplier of boxes of artefacts, including faiths and celebrations, themes, festivals and artefacts from named countries.

Articles of Faith, Resource House, Key Street, Bury BL9 6BU
Tel: 0161 763 6232
Email: ArticlesFaith@cs.com
Web: www.articlesoffaith.co.uk

Supplier of religious artefacts, videos, posters, CDs and tapes, dolls, books.

Chang's, 14 Pollards Hill East, London SW16 4UT
Tel: 020 8764 8377
Email: sallychang@fsworld.co.uk

Supplier of Chinese arts and crafts.

The Parrotfish Company, 51 North Street, Maldon, Essex CM9 5HJ
Tel: 01621 858940
Email: waterdunn@hotmail.com
Web: www.parrotfish.co.uk

Supplier of religious and cultural artefacts and fabrics from India.

Books

Ethos/Religion in Evidence, TTS, Monk Road, Alfreton, Derbyshire DE55 7RL
Tel: 0800 318686
Email: sales@tts-group.co.uk

Supplier mainly of books for RE and PSHE, but also artefacts, videos, posters.

Hibiscus Books, 122–6 High Road, London NW6 4HY
Tel: 020 7692 0643

Publisher of books and posters. Its Millennium People series depicts Black British achievers.

Kingscourt, Freepost PO Box 1427, London W6 9BR
Tel: 0800 317457
Email: enquiries@kingscourt.co.uk

Producer of Maths scheme, which includes Big Books depicting Maths from 65 cultures. The books cover Foundation to Year 5.

Mantra, 5 Alexandra Grove, London N12 8NU
Tel: 020 8445 5123
Email: info@mantrapublishing.com
Web: www.mantrapublishing.com

Publisher of dual-language books for Key Stages One and Two, books for young adults, multilingual friezes and signs, videos, CD-Roms.

Multicultural Books Ltd, PO Box 107, Greenford, Middlesex UB6 9YX
Tel: 020 8613 1978
Email: blossom@paublo.demon.co.uk
Web: www.multiculturalbooks.co.uk

Supplier of multicultural books.

Multicultural Book Services, Unit 33, Carlisle Business Centre, 60 Carlisle Road, Bradford BD8 8BD
Tel: 01274 544158
Email: aamirdarr@multiculturalbookservice.fsnet.co.uk

Supplier of dual-language books, big books, fiction and non-fiction, books for teachers.

Positive Identity, PO Box 17709, London SE6 4ZQ
Tel: 020 8314 0442
Email: info@positive-identity.com
Web: www.positive-identity.com

Supplier of books, dolls and games.

RDS, 8 Merton Road, London E17 9DE
Tel: 020 8521 6969
Email: r.desalvo@tesco.net
Web: www.members.tripod.co.uk/rds/index

Supplier of dual-language books, tapes and dictionaries.

Tamarind Books, PO Box 52, Northwood, Middlesex HA6 1UN
Tel: 020 8866 8808
Email: TamarindLTD@aol.com

Publisher of books, posters, puzzles depicting African Caribbean children and adults (KS 1–2).

Trentham Books Ltd, Westview House, 734 London Road, Oakhill, Stoke-on-Trent, Staffordshire ST4 5NP
Tel: 01782 745567
Email: tb@trentham-books.co.uk
Web: www.trentham-books.co.uk

Publisher of books for teachers on a range of issues concerned with inclusion and anti-racist education. Trentham also publishes the quarterly journal *Multicultural Teaching*.

Dolls

East West Education, 3 Keymer Gardens, Burgess Hill, West Sussex RH15 0AF
Tel: 01444 236322
Email: ewe@durai.demon.co.uk

Supplier of Indian dolls' clothes.

Noire Dolls Arts, 131 Hewitt Avenue, Wood Green, London N22 6QE
Tel 020 8881 1673

Producer of knitted dolls, dressed in African fabrics.

Positive Identity, PO Box 17709, London SE6 4ZQ

Tel: 020 8314 0442
Email: info@positive-identity.com
Web: www.positive-identity.com

Supplier of books, dolls and games.

Music

Acorn Percussion, Unit 33 Abbey Business Centre, Ingate Place, London SW8 3NS
Tel: 020 7720 2243
Email: acornpercussion@btinternet.com

Supplier of musical instruments from around the world.

World Music Network, 6 Abbeville Mews, 88 Clapham Park Road, London SW4 7BX
Tel: 020 7498 5252
Email: post@worldmusic.net
Web: www.worldmusic.net

Supplier of CDs of music by artists from around the world and sampler albums.

Software

Lingua, 4 Glenthorpe, Lamma Wells Road, Holmfirth HD9 2SP
Tel: 01484 689494
Email: enquiries@lingua-uk.com
Web: www.lingua-uk.com

Producer of multilingual software.

Websites

The following websites offer access to advice and tips on resources and support strategies for bilingual and minority ethnic pupils. Some encourage online networking as a means to share good practice.

The teacherworld website devised by Yasmin Valli at Leeds Metropolitan University is particularly useful in this respect. Yasmin Valli explains that online networks help to dissolve the professional isolation of teachers through the establishment of collective identities within online communities. Within the network, colleagues are able to share good practice and resources, offer each other advice and have a sense of belonging by participating in a community of shared interests. The development of a sense of belonging is particularly important for EMTAG staff, who may be working independently following the devolution of grant away from central service provision to individual schools. These websites provide a useful source of information to colleagues who have relatively little experience of working in multi-ethnic classrooms. The TES site offers especially useful tips on the inclusion of newly arrived migrant pupils.

www.teacherworld.org.uk
www.tes.co.uk/your-subject/subject-index.asp?subject=EAL
www.literarytrust.org.uk/Database/EALres.html
www.hants.gov.uk/blss
www.blss.portsmouth.sch.uk

References

Ainscow, M. (1999) *Understanding the Development of Inclusive Schools*. London: Falmer Press.

Alexander, R., Rose, J. and Woodhead, C. (1992) *Curriculum Organisation and Classroom Practice in Primary Schools: A Discussion Paper*. London: DfEE.

Barnes, D. (1976) *From Communication to Curriculum*. Harmondsworth: Penguin.

Blair, M. and Bourne, J. (1998) *Making the Difference: Teaching and Learning Strategies in Successful Multi-ethnic Schools*. London: DfEE.

Bourne, J. and McPake, J. (1991) *Partnership Teaching: Co-operative Teaching Strategies for English Language Support in Multilingual Classrooms*. London: HMSO.

Brent Language Service (1999) *Enriching Literacy: Text, Talk and Tales in Today's Classroom: A Practical Handbook for Multilingual Schools*. Stoke-on-Trent: Trentham Books.

Brown, B. (2000) 'Breaking the cycle of racism', *Early Years Educator*, vol. 4, no. 2 (August).

Brown, B. (2001) *Combating Discrimination: Persona Dolls in Action*. Stoke-on–Trent: Trentham Books.

Coelho, E. (1998) *Teaching and Learning in Multicultural Schools*. Clevedon: Multilingual Matters.

Commission for Racial Equality (1998) *Education and Training in Britain*. London: CRE.

Commission for Racial Equality (2001) *Statutory Code of Practice on the Duty to Promote Race Equality: A Guide for Schools*. London: CRE.

Corden, R. (2000) *Literacy and Learning Through Talk: Strategies for the Primary Classroom*. Buckingham: Open University Press.

Cummins, J. (1984) *Bilingualism and Special Education: Issues in Assessment Pedagogy*. Clevedon: Multilingual Matters.

DfEE/QCA (1999) *The National Curriculum: Handbook for Secondary Teachers in England*. London: DfEE and Qualifications and Curriculum Authority.

Dulay, H., Krashen, S. and Burt, M. (1982) *Language Two*. Oxford: Oxford University Press.

Fenton, S. (1999) *Ethnicity: Racism, Class and Culture*. Basingstoke: Macmillan.

Gaine, C. (1995) *Still No Problem Here*. Stoke-on-Trent: Trentham Books.

Galton, M., Hargreaves, L., Comber, C., Wall, D. and Pell, A. (1999) *Inside the Primary Classroom 20 Years On*. London: Routledge.

Galton, M., Simon, B. and Croll, P. (1980) *Inside the Primary Classroom*. London: Falmer Press.

Gardner, P. (1998) 'Writing: Creative Observation', *The Primary English Magazine*, vol. 4, no. 2.

Gardner, P. (2001) *Teaching and Learning in Multicultural Classrooms*. London: David Fulton Publishers.

Gillborn, D., and Mirza, H. (2000) *Educational Inequality: Mapping Race, Class and Gender – A Synthesis of Research Evidence*. London: Ofsted.

Jary, D. and Jary, J. (1991) *Dictionary of Sociology*. London: HarperCollins.

Jones, R. (1999) *Teaching Racism or Tackling It?: Multicultural Stories from White Beginning Teachers*. Stoke-on-Trent: Trentham Books.

Kincheloe, J.L. and Steinberg, S.R. (1997) *Changing Multiculturalism*. Buckingham: Open University Press.

Lunzer, E. and Gardner, K. (eds) (1979) *The Effective Uses of Reading*. London: Heinemann.

Macpherson, W. (1999) *The Stephen Lawrence Inquiry*. London: Stationery Office.

Maslow, A. H. (1968) *Towards a Psychology of Being*, 2nd edn. Princeton, N.J.: Van Nostrand.

Ofsted (1999) *Raising the Attainment of Minority Ethnic Pupils: School and LEA Responses*. London: Ofsted.

Robins, V. (1998) *The Invisible Professionals: Nursery Nurses Working in Schools*. Derby: Professional Association of Teachers.

Smith, F. (1994) *Writing and the Writer*. Hillsdale, N.J.: Erlbaum.

Troyna, B. and Hatcher, R. (1992) *Racism in Children's Lives*. London: Routledge.

TTA (2002) *Qualifying to Teach: Professional Standards for Qualified Teacher Status and Requirements for Initial Teacher Training*. London: Teacher Training Agency.

Vygotsky, L. S. (1962) *Thought and Language*. Cambridge, Mass.: MIT Press.

Yeomans, R. (1989) 'Sustaining a Partnership of Unequal Colleagues', *Early Years Journal*, vol. 10, no. 1.

Index